TO:

....

FROM:

....

DATE:

....

New Morning Mercies

DEVOTIONS & PRAYERS
FOR WOMEN

Print ISBN 979-8-89151-203-0

Compiled by Barbour Publishing, Inc.

Devotions and prayers are from: *Daily Wisdom for Women Devotional Collections*—2013, 2014, 2015, 2016, 2017, 2018, 2019, 2020, 2021, 2022, 2023, 2024, 2025.

Published by Barbour Publishing, Inc., 1810 Barbour Drive, Uhrichsville, Ohio 44683, www.barbourbooks.com

Our mission is to inspire the world with the life-changing message of the Bible.

Member of the Evangelical Christian Publishers Association

Printed in China.

New Morning Mercies

FOR YOUR BEAUTIFUL SOUL

The faithful love of the Lord never ends! His mercies never cease. Great is his faithfulness; his mercies begin afresh each morning. I say to myself, "The Lord is my inheritance; therefore, I will hope in him!"

LAMENTATIONS 3:22–24 NLT

The heavenly Father's mercies are new every morning, and this lovely devotional celebrates that truth. These more than 200 devotions will comfort, inspire, encourage, and infuse hope into your heart. Every page gifts you with these lovely reminders: God is good. . .He is faithful. . .He is love! Read on and immerse your spirit in inspiration and encouragement every day of the year.

Joy in the Morning

All who seek the Lord will praise him.
Their hearts will rejoice with everlasting joy.
Psalm 22:26 NLT

How grand God is! He knows how dependent we are on Him for the everyday joy we need to carry on. And every day, He provides us with beauty all around to cheer and help us.

It may come through the beauty of flowers or the bright blue sky—or maybe the white snow covering the trees of a glorious winter wonderland. It may be through the smile of a child or the grateful face of the one we care for. Each and every day, the Lord has a special gift to remind us of whose we are and to generate the joy we need to succeed.

In our own pain and frustration, there are times when our eyes don't see the beauty God sends. But if we ask, He'll show us. God is faithful to build us up with everything we need to serve Him with joy. What an awesome God we follow!

LORD GOD, I THANK YOU FOR YOUR JOY; I THANK YOU FOR PROVIDING IT EVERY DAY TO SUSTAIN ME. I WILL BE JOYFUL IN YOU.

Cultivating Contentment

I wait for the Lord, my whole being waits, and in his word I put my hope. I wait for the Lord more than watchmen wait for the morning, more than watchmen wait for the morning.
Psalm 130:5–6 niv

What are you waiting for—a job, a relationship, physical healing, financial provision? Whatever answer to prayer you are longing for, remember that often it's in the waiting that God performs His perfecting work on our character. Joseph waited for many years, serving in Pharaoh's house (even ending up in jail) before God promoted him. Abraham waited until he was a century old to see the child God had promised to him and Sarah decades before. God was still at work in both men's lives, though His actions and plans were hidden.

Maybe you've waited for God to come through, and so far, He hasn't. The word *advent* means "arrival or coming, especially of one which is awaited." Like the silence the people of Israel endured for 400 years between the last spoken prophetic word and the arrival of the Christ child, perhaps you've endured silence from God for so long that you think He's not there, not listening—or not inclined to come to your rescue.

No matter what you're going through, please know that God is for you, not against you. He aches with you. And He offers us a choice: Be chained in fear or changed by grace.

Which will you choose today?

FATHER, FORGIVE ME FOR DOUBTING YOUR LOVE AND MERCY. THANK YOU THAT YOU ARE FAITHFUL AND THAT YOU WILL PROVIDE FOR ME. I BELIEVE. . .HELP MY UNBELIEF.

Come and Find Me

I have wandered away like a lost sheep; come and find me.
PSALM 119:176 NLT

Sheep are funny creatures. Left to their own devices, they meander through fields, searching for the next choice mouthful. Their stomachs guide them. That's why they sometimes get themselves into precarious situations and often don't see their enemies until it's too late.

Have you ever acted like a ewe? Wandering through life, seeking to feed your desires? Looking for the next thing you think might satisfy you?

Everyone wanders away sometimes. And every time, the reason is stupid—just like it is for the sheep who willingly steps out of sight of her one and only protector.

Face it. There's no good argument for leaving the shepherd. He knows you. He's the only one who knows every thought you have ever had, every word you have ever said or left unsaid. And He still loves you and wants you to be with Him. Can you really think of a good reason to leave Him?

But undoubtedly you will. Everyone will stray. Everyone will turn their backs—again and again.

"Come and find me," you can pray. And He will. Your shepherd will come with grace and mercy. He will come and pick you up and take you back to the flock again. Maybe this time you will stay.

LORD, HELP ME TO UNDERSTAND THAT MY SAFEST PLACE IS WITH YOU. AMEN.

May We Never Forget

"When you cross the Jordan River and enter the land the LORD your God is giving you, set up some large stones and coat them with plaster. Write this whole body of instruction on them when you cross the river to enter the land the LORD your God is giving you—a land flowing with milk and honey, just as the LORD, the God of your ancestors, promised you."

DEUTERONOMY 27:2-3 NLT

Picture the Israelites crossing the Jordan River into the Promised Land. Can you see them scratching their heads as they listen to the Lord's last-minute instructions? Can you hear their questions: "Wait a minute, Lord. . .stones? Put them. . .where?"

Oh, but after the fact, when they looked back at the place where they crossed over, it all became crystal clear. What a tangible reminder of what the Lord had done! Those very stones stood as a memorial, a vivid reminder, so that they would never forget their deliverance story.

When God works miracles on our behalf, delivering us from our proverbial (and often very real) enemies, He longs for our trust to grow as we remember all He's done on our behalf. May we lift our hearts and hands in praise for all He's brought us through.

LORD, YOU'VE CARRIED ME THROUGH ROUGH SEASONS AND BROUGHT ME INTO NEW PLACES WHERE I CAN THRIVE IN YOU. MAY I NEVER LOSE MY SENSE OF WONDER OVER YOUR GRACE, PROVISION, AND LOVE. I TRUST YOU, FATHER. AMEN.

Weary Days

Why art thou cast down, O my soul? and why art thou disquieted in me? hope thou in God: for I shall yet praise him for the help of his countenance. O my God, my soul is cast down within me: therefore will I remember thee from the land of Jordan, and of the Hermonites, from the hill Mizar.

Psalm 42:5–6 KJV

It's easy for life's responsibilities and commitments to drag us down. Each day seems like a repeat of the day before. The morning alarm becomes our enemy, and the snooze button becomes our considerate companion. Our hard work often goes unappreciated. Nothing feels accomplished. Our souls yearn for something more.

If we accept it, God's constant goodness can be our delight. In the mornings, instead of our groaning and hiding beneath the pillows, God desires for us to communicate with Him. His voice could be the first one that we hear each day. As we roll over and stretch, we can then say, "I love You, God. Thank You for another day of life."

Our willingness to speak with God at the day's beginning shows our dependence on Him. We can't make it alone. It is a comforting truth that God never intended for us to trek through the day unaccompanied. He promises to be with us. He also promises His guidance and direction as we meet people and receive opportunities to serve Him.

Getting started is as simple as removing our heads from beneath the pillows and telling God good morning.

LORD, REFRESH MY SPIRIT AND GIVE ME JOY FOR TODAY'S ACTIVITIES. AMEN.

Great Expectations

Now there was a man in Jerusalem called Simeon, who was righteous and devout. He was waiting for the consolation of Israel, and the Holy Spirit was on him. It had been revealed to him by the Holy Spirit that he would not die before he had seen the Lord's Messiah.

Luke 2:25–26 NIV

Simeon was an old man. He was righteous and devout. But surely there were other old men hanging around the temple who were also righteous and devout. Of all the Pharisees and Sadducees nearby, of all the truly devoted, religious people of that day, why Simeon? Why did God choose this man to welcome His Son into the temple and proclaim His coming to all who would listen?

One key phrase offers a clue: "He was waiting for the consolation of Israel." In other words, Simeon knew God's promises, and he was looking for good things to happen.

What a lesson we can learn from this old saint! God has promised many good things to His people. But we often mope around, stressed and anxious, worried that things won't go well for us. Why do we do that? Like Simeon, we should wake up each morning looking for God to do great things. We should greet each new day expecting God to work, to fulfill His promises.

DEAR FATHER, THANK YOU FOR YOUR PROMISES. I KNOW YOU HAVE GOOD THINGS IN STORE. HELP ME TO WATCH AND WAIT, EXPECTING YOU TO DO GREAT THINGS EACH AND EVERY DAY. AMEN.

Precious Time with Him

I say to the L*ORD*, *"You are my God." Hear,* L*ORD*, *my cry for mercy. Sovereign* L*ORD*, *my strong deliverer, you shield my head in the day of battle.*

PSALM 140:6–7 NIV

Often we are distracted by life to the point that we are too busy to connect with the Lord.

Regardless of today's workload or your planned to-dos, resist the pressing urge to jump into your busyness first thing. Instead, determine to spend some time with the Lord.

Pour a cup of tea and sit in your favorite chair. Look out your window to whatever nature might surround you. Better yet, take a nice, leisurely walk around your neighborhood or in a park. Either way, begin to pray quietly. Stop for a moment to drink in your surroundings, the beauty that reflects your Creator.

If you are outside, notice that just as the air escaping your lips is normally unseen in other seasons, fall exposes the presence of God. Notice that those things that often are invisible seem to be shouting out God's presence with each step you take.

How wonderful that in these quiet moments, God takes every means to remind you that He cherishes the precious time you spend with Him.

LORD, FORGIVE ME FOR BEING DISTRACTED. I WILL MAKE TIME FOR YOU—ESPECIALLY TODAY. GIVE ME A VISIBLE GLIMPSE OF YOU.

Trusting Tower

The name of the Lord *is a strong tower;*
the righteous run to it and are safe.
Proverbs 18:10 NKJV

Words used to describe a tower are: tall, high structure, stronghold, or something strong enough to hold things such as water or food. When you were little, and you heard stories about princes and princesses, kings and queens, cops and robbers, did you imagine a tower to be like that—strong. . .immovable. . .unshakable?

Like a tower that stands tall and strong from the ground up, God is a tower to our faith. Jesus, when He died on a tree and rose again, became your strong tower as well. Everything that He did was enough to pay the penalty for your sins and empower you to live a life in Him. All you need to do is approach His throne of grace. Hebrews 9:28 (GW) says, "Likewise, Christ was sacrificed once to take away the sins of humanity, and after that he will appear a second time. This time he will not deal with sin, but he will save those who eagerly wait for him."

As you trust in Elohim—which is the plural form of *El*, meaning "strong one"—thank God and Jesus for what They have done for you. And trust that Christ is coming again for you.

LORD, WHEN I NEED TO TRUST YOU MORE, I WANT TO RUN TO YOU MORE. THANK YOU FOR BEING MY REFUGE, MY MIGHTY TOWER OF STRENGTH.

Rocky Road, Steady Faith

Blessed be the LORD forever! Amen and Amen.

PSALM 89:52 ESV

The psalms cover a lot of ground—from laments to worship. They show the human side of faith as God's people try to live out their beliefs each day, even when they wonder about what's happening. Psalms 88 and 89 are examples of this tension.

The writer of Psalm 88 didn't know why he had been plagued by an illness. "O LORD, why do you reject me?" he wrote. "Why do you turn your face from me?" (Psalm 88:14 NLT). The writer of Psalm 89 had a question too. He knew God's promises about Israel, but he didn't see God's promises being fulfilled, and he asked, "Lord, where is your unfailing love? You promised it to David with a faithful pledge" (Psalm 89:49 NLT).

Yet despite uncertainty, both psalmists chose to trust God to work *everything* out. Their situations may not have been explained, but they continued to turn to God: "O LORD, I cry out to you. I will keep on pleading day by day" (Psalm 88:13 NLT). What God promised may have seemed unlikely, but he still believed: "I will sing of the LORD's unfailing love forever! . . . Your faithfulness is as enduring as the heavens" (Psalm 89:1–2 NLT). Both psalmists chose faith. What do you choose?

MY WORLD MIGHT BE STRETCHED BY QUESTIONS,
BUT I CHOOSE TO PUT MY FAITH IN YOU,
BLESSED LORD. AMEN AND AMEN!

The Gift of Manna

They asked, and He brought quail,
and satisfied them with the bread of heaven.
PSALM 105:40 NASB

Who wouldn't welcome the delivery of free bread on their doorstep each morning? Well, the Israelites had it made, and they still complained. "Same old, same old" they'd have cried out in today's vernacular. A one-day supply of this sticky, white, honey-flavored nourishment, called manna, covered the ground each morning. After gathering it, the Israelites ground it between two millstones or beat it with a mortar, boiled it in a pot, and made cakes with it. The taste was similar to cakes baked with oil (Numbers 11:8). However, after forty years, the thought of waking up to this substance didn't exactly entice them to crawl out of their tents in anticipation.

After their repeated complaints, God gave the Israelites some quail to eat (Numbers 11:31). No matter how God cared for them, the Israelites found something to criticize.

Another life-giving bread is symbolically offered to us under the new covenant. Jesus said, "I am the living bread that came down out of heaven; if anyone eats from this bread, he will live forever; and the bread which I will give for the life of the world also is My flesh" (John 6:51 NASB). Christ Himself compared the two breads: "This is the bread that came down out of heaven, not as the fathers ate and died; the one who eats this bread will live forever" (John 6:58 NASB).

LORD, I LONG TO LIVE FOREVER IN YOUR GLORIOUS PRESENCE.

Talking to the Father

The prayer of a righteous person is powerful and effective.
James 5:16 niv

We have all had those inevitable days when we are exhausted or discouraged and it seems too hard to carry on. We might feel as dry as the desert sand, with nothing left to give. This is a time when we could use nourishment for our souls.

The prophet Zechariah said, "Ask the Lord for rain in the springtime, and he will answer with lightning and showers" (10:1 tlb). Matthew Henry explained this scripture: "Spiritual blessings had been promised. . . . We must in our prayers ask for mercies in their proper time. The Lord would make bright clouds, and give showers of rain. . .[when we] seek the influences of the Holy Spirit, in faith and by prayer, through which the blessings held forth in the promises are obtained."

When these times hit, use "knee mail." Don't just "tweet" a short sigh to the Lord, but carve out some time to pray, to praise, and to petition our heavenly Father for strength to carry on. He is faithful to answer our pleas and send refreshment to our hearts. It could be in the form of a restful night's sleep, a friend or relative to exhort and encourage, or a stranger's greeting. We never know how the Lord will answer our petitions, but He will answer. God's inbox is never too full.

DEAR LORD, HOW I LONG FOR YOUR PRESENCE.
FATHER, HEAR MY PRAYERS THIS DAY;
EXTEND YOUR HAND OF MERCY TO ME. AMEN.

God's Partner

In everything we do, we show that we are true ministers of God.
2 Corinthians 6:4 NLT

When you turn on the television to glimpse the evening news, you are immediately reminded of the fallen world you live in. Danger, calamity, and terror are all around, yet you have hope in God's mercy because you know who you are.

- You are God's partner (see 2 Corinthians 6:1).
- You patiently endure troubles, hardships, and calamities of all sorts and sizes (see verse 4).
- You know that God's power is working in you (see verse 7).
- Your heart may ache, but you have eternal joy (see verse 10).
- You may be poor, but you give spiritual riches to others (see verse 10).
- You may own little but have everything (see verse 10).
- You have no lack of love within you, even though others withhold their love from you (see verse 12).

In other words, as God's partner, you see the world with His eyes. You know He's living in you. He's your safety zone. As you abide in Him, nothing can touch you.

FATHER, THANK YOU FOR ALLOWING ME TO BE YOUR PARTNER AS I ABIDE IN YOU.

Hold On Tight

Let us hold tightly without wavering to the hope we affirm, for God can be trusted to keep his promise. Let us think of ways to motivate one another to acts of love and good works.

HEBREWS 10:23-24 NLT

Take a few minutes to reflect on the word *trust*. More specifically, think about the relationships you have in your life right now. Then think about the relationships that have drifted or changed over the years. What is one of the characteristics that has helped you maintain a solid relationship with someone?

Chances are, trust is an important quality for you. Trust helps build a foundation and gives you an assurance that your words, and the words of others, are safe. Proverbs 18:21 (NLT) says: "The tongue can bring death or life; those who love to talk will reap the consequences." As Solomon wrote these words, he recalled a truth about relationships. Words can hurt or heal. Your words, and those of others, are powerful. But God's are the most powerful of all.

Hebrews 10:23 encourages you to hold tightly, without wavering, to the hope you have because God can be trusted to keep His promises. In other words, God can be trusted to keep His word. Therefore, trust and hold on tight to Him.

FATHER, I'M SO GRATEFUL FOR THE POWER AND HOPE FOUND IN YOUR WORDS. GIVE ME YOUR GRACE TO HOLD ON TIGHT TO YOUR PROMISES.

In the Midst of Trouble

Though I am surrounded by troubles, you will protect me. . . . The Lord will work out his plans for my life—for your faithful love, O Lord, endures forever.

Psalm 138:7–8 NLT

Sometimes when we feel the walls of a tough situation closing in on us, we lose sight of God. We fail to see that He is with us absolutely everywhere—no matter what situation we find ourselves in or put ourselves in—and He never stops intervening in our lives. David expressed wonder at the thought, saying, "You know everything I do. . . . You go before me and follow me. You place your hand of blessing on my head. Such knowledge is too wonderful for me, too great for me to understand!" (Psalm 139:3, 5–6 NLT).

David could go no place where God wasn't already present, waiting to shepherd him. "Where can I go from your Spirit? Where can I flee from your presence?" David asked. "If I rise on the wings of the dawn, if I settle on the far side of the sea, even there your hand will guide me, your right hand will hold me fast" (verses 7, 9–10 NIV).

Are troubles making you claustrophobic? Shift your focus to the one who is ever present, ever faithful, and ever working out His plans for you.

LORD, YOU'VE NOT ABANDONED ME IN MY TROUBLES. HELP ME SEE YOU. AMEN.

Powerful One

He who forms the mountains, who creates the wind, and who reveals his thoughts to mankind, who turns dawn to darkness, and treads on the heights of the earth—the LORD God Almighty is his name.

AMOS 4:13 NIV

Ever pondered the power of our Lord God Almighty? Meditating on God's power can soothe our biggest worries and calm our deepest fears.

The Word of God speaks often of His power—we know He created our universe in less than a week. But if that's too much to comprehend, consider the enormity of a single mountain or ocean. Those vast, mighty things came into being simply by God's voice—and they're only a tiny fraction of everything He made. What power!

The Lord opens the morning curtains to reveal the dawn and pulls the sky shades back at night to bring darkness. He plots the course of the wind, arranges for rainfall, and causes grass, crops, and trees to grow. He feeds the gigantic whales of the ocean, and every tiny little bird. If our Lord has enough knowledge and power to handle these jobs, surely He can (and will!) look after us.

Problems that seem insurmountable to us are simply a breath to Him. Let's not be anxious today—God holds each one of us in the palm of His hand.

LORD GOD, YOU ARE MY PROVIDER. THANK YOU FOR HOLDING SUCH POWER—AND FOR CHOOSING ME TO BE YOUR CHILD. PLEASE GIVE ME A GREATER UNDERSTANDING OF WHO YOU ARE, HELPING ME TO REMEMBER THAT YOU, THE LORD GOD ALMIGHTY, LOVE ME.

An Extravagant God

Return to the Lord your God, for he is merciful and compassionate, slow to get angry and filled with unfailing love.

Joel 2:13 NLT

There are often times when we are exhausted and discouraged and we allow our minds to roam to dark places. Despair and disappointment set in. A woe-is-me attitude prevails within us. How is it possible to rise from the doldrums? How do we continue? We turn our faces toward the Lord God and know He is in control.

Scripture tells of God's mercy and loving-kindness. It speaks out and urges us to come back to God. This doesn't necessarily mean a change of circumstances, but a change of heart. This change is a choice we intentionally make. It's not necessary to be in a church building or a revival when we make this choice. While many changes happen there, ours can be in our closets, cars, or offices. We reach inwardly to the Highest and ask for His mercy. And scripture says He is merciful and full of grace. He hears our prayers.

Focusing on the negative, choosing despair, doesn't bring life. Voluntarily focusing on Jesus will. Praise Him for all your blessings: They are there; look for them. Some might be tiny, others magnificent. But they're all because of our Lord Jesus Christ. He is a most patient God and extravagant in His love.

O HEAVENLY FATHER, I PRAISE YOUR NAME. YOU ARE EXTRAVAGANT IN YOUR LOVE, AND I AM GRATEFUL FOR ALL YOU'VE DONE. AMEN.

Whispers of Love

I am praying to you because I know you will answer, O God. Bend down and listen as I pray. Show me your unfailing love in wonderful ways.

Psalm 17:6–7 NLT

Like the psalmist David, you probably have a day now and then when you feel empty or alone. Maybe you struggle to keep nagging, negative thoughts at bay. In many of his psalms, David shared his challenges to keep his negative thoughts from imprisoning him. At first he would give in, but then as he remembered God's faithfulness, he was able to break the tentacles of doubt.

When those self-assaulting thoughts come to the forefront of your mind, refuse the lies and focus on the many times God has come through for you. He loves you with an everlasting love (Jeremiah 31:3). He is faithful (Hebrews 10:23). He will never leave you (Hebrews 13:5). He is with you always (Matthew 28:20). He has given you a future and a hope (Jeremiah 29:11).

Remind yourself of God's Word, just as David did, and doing so will bring you back to your spiritual senses. As the light of God's truth makes its way in, you will begin to break free. His promises remove the prison bars of doubt so that you can hope again.

God is there—as He has always been. Listen quietly for the gentle whispers of His unfailing love.

THANK YOU, GOD, FOR YOUR WHISPERS OF LOVE. WHEN NEGATIVE THOUGHTS CHALLENGE ME TO GIVE IN AND DOUBT, I WILL REMEMBER YOUR MERCY, COMPASSION, AND FAITHFULNESS. LORD, HEAR MY PRAYER.

Nightwatch

I wait for the Lord, my soul doth wait, and in his word do I hope. My soul waiteth for the Lord more than they that watch for the morning: I say, more than they that watch for the morning.

Psalm 130:5–6 KJV

Waiting is a fundamental part of the human experience.

A mother waits nine long months to hold her child.

A father sits by the phone, hoping against hope his wayward child will call home.

The insomniac longs for sleep and waits for a reason to get up.

The Christian waits for the Lord to act. For His return. For the day that faith will be sight.

Job understood that kind of waiting. In his grief, he said, "If only you would set me a time and then remember me!" (Job 14:13 NIV). He had absolute confidence that day would come. "You *will call* and I will answer you" (Job 14:15 NIV, emphasis added).

The psalmist matched Job's confidence because with God comes forgiveness (see Psalm 130:4). His love never fails.

With that confidence, wait for the morning.

ETERNAL GOD, WHEN I WAIT IN THE DARK, YOU PREPARE THE SUNRISE OF MY NEW DAY. WHAT I NOW GLIMPSE IN THE SHADOWS, I WILL ONE DAY SEE REVEALED IN THE FULL LIGHT. I THANK YOU FOR THE TIMES YOUR FLASHLIGHT SHOWS ME PIECES OF THAT FINAL COMPLETE PICTURE. AMEN.

Favorite Child

"Before I formed you in the womb I knew you, before you were born I set you apart; I appointed you as a prophet to the nations."

JEREMIAH 1:5 NIV

Expectant parents often wonder what their future bundle of joy will look like. Whom will he most resemble? Will the baby have hair? How much will he weigh? There are so many questions. Though both parents had a part in the creation of this new little being, they are clueless as to exactly what kind of person their offspring will become.

This was not the case with God when He called Jeremiah, who was already a young man. God wanted Jeremiah to know how vital he was. He had Jeremiah earmarked as special long before he was even born. God called him to play an important role in His plan.

God the Father knows you as well. You too are one of His blessed children. He knew you long before you were born, and He knows you now. He calls to you and has you earmarked to play a role in His plan. You just need to be receptive to His call, to listen intently for His instruction, to know, believe, and trust that you are vital to His plan.

DEAR LORD, HELP ME REMEMBER THAT I AM SPECIAL TO YOU. OPEN MY EARS TO YOUR VOICE. I, YOUR FAITHFUL AND LOVING CHILD, AM HERE TO SERVE YOU, TO ANSWER YOUR CALL, AND TO SPREAD YOUR WORD.

One Day at a Time

Blessed be the Lord, who daily loadeth us with benefits, even the God of our salvation.

Psalm 68:19 KJV

There's a reason why the Lord's Prayer teaches us to ask for daily bread. We tend to forget about yesterday's provision in the crunch of today's needs. God calls us to a childlike faith, one that basks in the provisions of the moment and forgets yesterday's disappointments and tomorrow's worries.

Think about small children. A toddler may cry when another child knocks him down and takes away his ball. The tears disappear when his mother hugs him and gives him a kiss. His joy in the expression of his mother's love obliterates his disappointment about the toy. Later he returns to the ball with fresh enthusiasm. He lives in the moment.

God always provides for us. Benefits overflow the shopping carts of our lives every single day. But He only gives us what we need for today, not for tomorrow. He knows that we need those benefits like a daily vitamin. By tomorrow, even later today, we may forget all that God has done for us. The Bible verse that spoke to us this morning feels empty by afternoon.

God gives us blessings every day so that we still have what we need after we have spent ourselves on life's disappointments.

FATHER, YOU GIVE US BREAD DAILY. WE PRAISE YOU FOR YOUR CONSTANT CARE AND ASK THAT YOU WILL TRAIN OUR EYES TO FOCUS ON YOUR BLESSINGS, NOT ON OUR FAILINGS. AMEN.

Bill of Rights

But to as many as did receive and welcome Him, He gave the right [the authority, the privilege] to become children of God, that is, to those who believe in (adhere to, trust in, and rely on) His name.

JOHN 1:12 AMP

The United States has a bill of rights that lays out guarantees of personal freedoms and limits the government's power. As US citizens, we observe these amendments to maintain an orderly and acceptable society. As Christians, we also have rights.

Scripture states we have been given "rights" as children of God. We have the "right" to receive direction from the Holy Spirit (Romans 8:14–17). We have the "right" to make our requests known to God (Philippians 4:6). We have the "right" to personal freedom from sin (Galatians 5:1). And we have the "right" to rule in our sphere of authority on the word of our testimony (Revelation 12:11).

Are you a child of the King? Are you an heir to the throne who can lay claim to these rights? Lift up your eyes to the heavens and declare your desire to become one of the family of God. He hears you. His Word says you can trust in His goodness and mercy, His loving-kindness. Reach out this day and receive your gift of salvation.

FATHER GOD, I WANT TO BE ONE OF YOUR CHILDREN, NOT JUST TO ATTAIN THE "RIGHTS" BUT TO UNDO WRONGS AND SIN IN MY LIFE. OPEN MY EYES THAT I MAY SEE. AMEN.

Jesus Does the Unexpected

When the Lord saw her, his heart overflowed with compassion. "Don't cry!" he said.
Luke 7:13 NLT

A crowd followed Jesus and His disciples when they reached the village of Nain. There He noticed the funeral procession of a young man, a widow's only son.

When Jesus saw her, He couldn't help but be deeply touched by her grief and her dire situation. Without her asking anything of Him, He first told her not to cry and then, amazingly, brought her dead son back to life! After the boy sat up and began to talk, "Jesus gave him back to his mother" (Luke 7:15 NLT).

When you are at your wits' end, when it looks like there's no hope for you, when you find yourself walking in a daze, struck with sadness, remember this story.

Know that Jesus sees what you are going through. His heart overflows with compassion for you.

So don't cry. Don't be discouraged. Don't despair. Don't grieve. Only believe. At the last minute, Jesus just may surprise you beyond anything you ever imagined or expected and turn your entire life around by doing the impossible.

JESUS, YOU NEVER CEASE TO AMAZE ME. THANK YOU FOR THE REMINDER THAT I NEED NEVER DESPAIR, FOR YOU SEE WHAT IS HAPPENING IN MY LIFE. I FEEL YOUR LOVE AND COMPASSION SURROUNDING ME! I WILL NOT GRIEVE—ONLY BELIEVE.

Return to Him

"So give to the people this Message from God-of-the-Angel-Armies: 'Come back to me and I'll come back to you.'"

Zechariah 1:3 MSG

There are times when we feel distant from God. Our busy lives are full of distractions, pulling our focus away from Him and toward things that seem important at the moment. It can be a slow, subtle slipping away, and then one day we look up and realize that perhaps our times with God are few and far between. This is a ploy of the enemy of our souls to detour us from relationship with God.

The verse above is an encouraging reminder that God wants His people to return to Him—and that we all have the power to do so. In fact, He wants us to return to Him even when we feel we don't deserve His favor or forgiveness.

Take a few moments and look at your relationship with God. Do you feel distant from Him? Are there things you need to bring before Him—things that might be getting in the way of your willingness to fully and completely surrender to Him?

Zechariah 1:3 is a promise. Return to God—and He'll return to you.

HEAVENLY FATHER, THANK YOU FOR YOUR CONSTANT PURSUIT OF A RELATIONSHIP WITH ME. TODAY I RETURN TO YOU AND FULLY SURRENDER ALL OF MY LIFE TO YOUR LORDSHIP.

The Fiery Furnace

But suddenly, Nebuchadnezzar jumped up in amazement and exclaimed to his advisers, "Didn't we tie up three men and throw them into the furnace?" "Yes, Your Majesty, we certainly did," they replied. "Look!" Nebuchadnezzar shouted. "I see four men, unbound, walking around in the fire unharmed! And the fourth looks like a god!"

DANIEL 3:24–25 NLT

When Shadrach, Meshach, and Abednego refused to bow down to King Nebuchadnezzar's image, they knew they were probably going to die at the king's hands. Regardless, they could not ignore their consciences. They could not—would not—bow down to an idol.

Because of their courage and faithfulness, God spared them from death. They emerged from the fiery furnace without so much as the smell of smoke on them.

Perhaps you've been through a few fiery furnace experiences in your life too. You've paid a heavy price for choosing your faith over the lifestyle you once knew. But God is faithful. You have emerged without a hair singed. And just like those three Hebrew boys were not alone, you have not been alone either.

I'VE NEVER BEEN ALONE IN THE FIERY TRIALS, LORD. YOU'VE BEEN RIGHT THERE BESIDE ME, PROTECTING, DEFENDING, AND SAVING. I'M SO GRATEFUL. AMEN.

Sleep on It

It is of the Lord's mercies that we are not consumed, because his compassions fail not. They are new every morning: great is thy faithfulness.
Lamentations 3:22–23 KJV

"Sleep on it." Researchers have found that to be sound advice. They believe that sleep helps people sort through facts, thoughts, and memories, providing a clearer look at the big picture upon waking. Sleep also separates reality from emotions like fear and worry, which can cloud our thinking and interfere with rational decision-making.

Scientifically speaking, sleep is good medicine. For Christians, the biological effects of sleep are outweighed by the spiritual benefits of the new day God gives us. At the end of an exhausting day, after the worries and the pressures of life have piled high, we may lie down, feeling as though we can't take another moment of stress. But God's Word tells us that His great mercy will keep our worries and problems from consuming us.

Through the never-ending compassion of God, His faithfulness is revealed afresh each morning. We can rise with renewed vigor. We can eagerly anticipate the new day, leaving behind the concerns of yesterday.

HEAVENLY FATHER, THANK YOU FOR GIVING ME A NEW MEASURE OF YOUR MERCY AND COMPASSION EACH DAY SO THAT MY CONCERNS DON'T CONSUME ME. I REST IN YOU AND I LAY MY BURDENS AT YOUR FEET.

His Delight

"The Lord your God is with you, the Mighty Warrior who saves. He will take great delight in you; in his love he will no longer rebuke you, but will rejoice over you with singing."
Zephaniah 3:17 niv

Delight. What a wonderful word! The connotations of enjoyment and pleasure, joy and gladness. You are usually delighted when something has pleased you. Maybe it's the song of a bird; the chatter of your child; or simply a quiet, starry night that soothes your senses and fills your heart with satisfaction.

Scripture tells us the Lord will take delight in us and will rejoice over us with singing. Imagine that! The very mighty warrior of the universe relishing His creation. And that creation is you. It's hard to imagine when we have our dirty faces or are out of sorts that He could care for us at all. But it's true. Our God saves and loves. Our God is truth and mercy. He loves His children.

Take a deep breath and carve out some time to appreciate and bask in the truth of the Bible. God loves *you* and He delights in *you*. You are the apple of His eye. Reach out a hand to Him this day, knowing full well He will interlace His fingers with yours and never let go. Selah. Pause and reflect.

FATHER GOD, HOW I LOVE YOU. I DO NOT UNDERSTAND THE DEPTH AND BREADTH OF YOUR LOVE FOR ME, BUT I AM EVER SO GRATEFUL. AMEN.

Promises Fulfilled

Not one of all the LORD's *good promises to Israel failed; every one was fulfilled.*

JOSHUA 21:45 NIV

When was the last time you broke a promise? If you are like most people, it does happen from time to time, and undoubtedly more often than you would like.

Sometimes it's very hard to keep promises. Circumstances interfere. People, places, times, and availability change. You can't control all the factors, and so that promise you made suddenly slips out of your hands.

But God's promises are not like yours. He does not make promises that He cannot keep. And He keeps every promise that comes from His lips.

Do you know what promises God has made to you? Read His Word. Search for the promises of love and compassion, forgiveness and grace, reward and suffering. For He does not just promise good things will come. He also tells you that you will have trouble. You will be tempted. You will suffer for His name. But like the Israelites who had struggled for so long and spent so much time fighting their way into the Promised Land, you will also find rest on every side. If you stay with Him, He will rescue you and bring you to a land of peace. It's a promise.

GOD, I WANT TO REMEMBER YOUR PROMISES.
HELP ME ALSO TO KEEP MY WORD. AMEN.

God's Spirit in You

And because we are his children, God has sent the Spirit of his Son into our hearts, prompting us to call out, "Abba, Father." Now you are no longer a slave but God's own child. And since you are his child, God has made you his heir.

GALATIANS 4:6–7 NLT

Imagine you live in a large and beautiful home. You throw open the door. Walking in confidently, you call out with anticipation, "Daddy!" You know your Father is always there waiting for you. He's your Abba and delights to draw you, His precious child, near. He's never busy or tired, irritable or critical, but loving and kind. The way that you can enter and be accepted is proof you're not a slave but His daughter, welcomed with open arms.

Your Father has put a part of Himself, His Spirit, in you so that you'll never be alone. No matter how far you travel or what circumstances you're in, you have a part of Him closer than your heartbeat.

This is your true reality. You have been adopted by the most generous of all fathers and nothing can separate you from His love. Not only that, but everything He owns is yours!

Do you have needs? Bring them to your Abba Father. Do you have problems or concerns? Abba Father longs to help you. Spend time each day in the presence of your true Father.

ABBA FATHER, THANK YOU FOR MAKING ME YOUR OWN BELOVED CHILD.

The Lightness of Joy

He gets angry once in a while, but across a lifetime there is only love. The nights of crying your eyes out give way to days of laughter. . . . You changed wild lament into whirling dance; you ripped off my black mourning band and decked me with wildflowers.

PSALM 30:5, 11 MSG

Because you have God in your life, any sorrows you may suffer are transient, temporary. But the joy you have in God, in Jesus, and in the Spirit is persistent, eternal. And all you can do is laugh! For you know that your tears will fade. They will quickly dry up in the light of the morning. You'll find yourself willingly and easily praising God for bringing you out of the darkness of troubles and sorrow and back into the peace and lightness of joy.

How wonderful that after you pray to God, relating all your worries and woes, He turns things around for you. He changes your funeral dirge into a song and dance of celebration. He tears off your black mourning band and showers you with flowers. Next thing you know, you're bursting into songs of thanksgiving and praise of Him.

If you find yourself in the depths of sorrow and despair, go to the one who can pull you up out of darkness and into the joy of the morning light.

LORD, AS I PRAY, TAKE AWAY MY SORROWS OF THE NIGHT AND LEAD ME WITH THE JOY OF YOUR MORNING LIGHT. AMEN.

Mirror Image

Behold, thou art fair, my love; behold,
thou art fair; thou hast doves' eyes.
SONG OF SOLOMON 1:15 KJV

Getting up in the morning and looking in the mirror can be tough. The glass reflects back our exact image with all the blemishes in plain sight. In our eyes, the flaws stand out. Instead of seeing any beauty, we focus on the imperfections. The longer we consider them, the more pronounced they become. Before long, we see only ugliness in ourselves.

No matter how hard we try, when the focus is on self, we see shortcomings. Beauty treatments, plastic surgery, makeup, beautiful clothing—nothing helps. There is no way to cover the flaws we see. Our outlook even affects how others view us.

Our only hope is to see ourselves through a different mirror. We must remember that as we grow as Christians, we take on the characteristics of Christ. The more we become like Him, the more beautiful we are in our own eyes and to those around us.

When God looks at us as Christians, He sees the reflection of Christ. He sees us as very beautiful. God loves to behold us when we are covered in Christ. The mirror image He sees has none of the blemishes or imperfections—only the beauty.

O, GOD, THANK YOU FOR BEHOLDING ME AS BEING FAIR AND VALUABLE. HELP ME TO SEE MYSELF THROUGH YOUR EYES. AMEN.

Can You Relate?

You turned my wailing into dancing; you removed my sackcloth and clothed me with joy, that my heart may sing your praises and not be silent. LORD *my God, I will praise you forever.*

PSALM 30:11–12 NIV

David knew times of trouble, and he also knew what it meant to be relieved of trouble. He experienced want and he experienced abundance. He hid in fear of losing his life to a king that he knew hated him. . .and later, he danced with joy, praising God, amazed at God's provision and protection. Can you relate? You probably have never been chased by a king and his armies. But every life is full of ups and downs. There will be times when all you can hope to do is survive in the shelter of the Lord's wings. You know He is there, but you cannot sense His presence. You trust Him, but you don't know how in the world He will turn things around. Just keep trusting. Just keep believing. Just keep praying. David cried out to the Lord for mercy. Not just this psalm but many others are filled with David's pleas to the Lord. God is faithful to hear your prayers. Just as He turned David's sorrow into joy, He can do the same for you.

FATHER, I ASK YOU TO TURN MY WEEPING INTO LAUGHTER. TEACH ME TO PRAISE YOU NO MATTER MY CIRCUMSTANCES. AMEN.

Wilderness Days

So he said, "I have been very zealous for the LORD God of hosts; for the children of Israel have forsaken Your covenant, torn down Your altars, and killed Your prophets with the sword. I alone am left; and they seek to take my life."

1 KINGS 19:10 NKJV

After the Lord's triumph at Mount Carmel, Elijah spent forty days in the wilderness, despondent beyond belief, thinking he would soon die at the wicked hands of Ahab and Jezebel. Despite all of his work for God, all Elijah saw was the death of God's prophets, and God's people going wayward. He cried out, "It is enough! Now, LORD, take my life, for I am no better than my fathers!" (1 Kings 19:4 NKJV).

Instead of God giving Elijah a pep talk—"Remember all My miracles? My ravens feeding you by the brook? Get back in the game, Elijah!"—He sent an angel to sustain him in his grief. At the end of the forty days, God showed His servant His nearness in a still, small voice after the earthquakes and the wind and fire.

Maybe you have beaten yourself up for not doing more or being more for God. Or maybe you feel like your efforts go unseen or your resources are exhausted. But during your wilderness days, your compassionate God is by your side, and He always has more grace than you expect.

LORD, THANK YOU THAT YOU ARE NEAR ON MY WILDERNESS DAYS.

In God We Trust

Teach those who are rich in this world not to be proud and not to trust in their money, which is so unreliable. Their trust should be in God, who richly gives us all we need for our enjoyment.

1 Timothy 6:17 NLT

The value of the dollar goes up and down. Banks swell. Banks fail. The productivity of nations rises and falls. Surpluses cause hopes to multiply. Deficits cause longstanding depression.

The meaning of wealth changes all the time. You cannot trust it. You cannot build dreams on it. You cannot live fully on it.

Instead, put your trust in God. God does not shift in value depending on the stock market, or the price of oil, or what battles are raging in faraway lands. No amount of human insecurity can touch God's everlasting consistency. And God is not just our Creator, not just our sustainer, not just our Redeemer—He is our provider. And He is our friend. He knows everything that we need, long before we need it. He knows everything that will please and delight us, even before we realize our need to be delighted. He is our loving, generous, gracious Father, ever ready to supply us with good gifts—even though we never did a thing to deserve them.

Why wouldn't we trust Him?

FATHER GOD, HELP ME NOT TO PUT MY TRUST IN EARTHLY RICHES THAT WILL FADE. HELP ME REMEMBER THAT ALL I EVER NEED IS YOU. AMEN.

"Nothing to Fear Here"

The guards at the tomb were scared to death. They were so frightened, they couldn't move. The angel spoke to the women: "There is nothing to fear here."

MATTHEW 28:4–5 MSG

The morning after Jesus' death on the cross, two women—Mary Magdalene and the other Mary—head to Jesus' tomb to keep vigil there. Suddenly, as the earth shakes, an angel of God descends from heaven. He rolls the rock away from the tomb entrance, then sits there on top of the boulder. The men guarding the tomb are so afraid, they freeze.

The angel begins speaking to the women, saying, "Don't be afraid. Don't be alarmed. All is well. I know you're looking for Jesus. He's not here but was raised, just as He said He would be."

Once he's calmed down the Marys, the angel tells them to tell the other believers that Jesus is alive and will meet up with them in Galilee. So the women run off, filled with joy. When they meet Jesus along the way, He too tells them not to be afraid but to go and tell the others to meet Him in Galilee.

The message Jesus gave the women at the tomb is the same message He gives you. Don't allow anything to shake you up. Don't fear anything or anyone. Simply do as Jesus has told you to do, with joy in every step.

LORD JESUS, HELP ME TO LOOK FOR YOU IN ALL THINGS, TO STAY CALM, AND GO YOUR WAY IN JOY. AMEN.

Did God Say. . . ?

For we walk by faith, not by sight.
2 CORINTHIANS 5:7 NASB

The more complex life becomes, the easier it is to lose our perspective.

Maybe we begin to feel that we aren't supposed to be in our current roles after all. There must be someone else who can do a better job, who can handle all the stuff that comes up, who can do it more graciously than we can. Did God really say we should do this?

This is the time faith really comes into play. God *has* given us the task—and we must believe that not only has He asked us to do this job, He's also given us an abundance of mental, emotional, and physical supply. And not just once, but over and over every morning.

Rarely can we see our way clearly, but we can believe that God has the situation under His perfect control. We can believe that He will work it for His glory and for the good of ourselves and those around us.

As we learn to become more and more dependent on God, we trust Him more and more. Our faith, though it may have begun as the size of a mustard seed, will grow into a mighty tree.

LORD, I THANK YOU FOR CHOOSING ME TO WORK WITH YOU. GIVE ME THE FAITH I NEED TO SEE YOUR HAND IN EVERYDAY CIRCUMSTANCES AND TO ASK YOU FOR THE HELP I NEED.

Merciful Heavens!

I love the L*ORD*, *for he heard my voice; he heard my cry for mercy.*
PSALM 116:1 NIV

The days when nothing goes according to plan are frustrating beyond belief—even worse are the unexpected surprises. Summer storms bring down power lines, the computer crashes before important work is saved, a fresh pot of coffee splatters on the floor. No one was planning to spend the day huddled indoors listening to raging winds. The frazzled engineer still has to turn in her report by five p.m., and that whole kitchen needs mopped *before* going out for that much-needed cup of joe.

It's a good thing our heavenly Father is compassionate toward His children. Heaven knows we need mercy when even a small thing going wrong can ruin our thankful attitudes for the day, and we definitely need His kindness when we stagger under huge disappointments.

Thankfully, our Father is never surprised at what happens, because all events fit in with His eternal plan (Romans 8:28). He knows His children can't see all the details, but He does know how much they can handle (1 Corinthians 10:13). Best of all, they can call on Him to shower down compassion upon the situation. "Mercy, Father! I can't handle this alone." "Mercy, Lord Jesus! Lift this burden—it's so heavy." The psalmist praises God for hearing and answering his prayer for mercy. God is more generous with His mercy than we suspect—ask Him in faith, and see.

FATHER GOD, I LOVE YOU BECAUSE YOU KEEP POURING OUT MERCY UPON ME WHEN I NEED IT. HELP ME CONTINUALLY DRAW MY STRENGTH FROM YOU. AMEN.

Keep Holding On

He shall regard the prayer of the destitute,
and shall not despise their prayer.
PSALM 102:17 NKJV

After lamenting, the psalmist continues his prayer and expresses his expectation that he will see the Lord's goodness—that God "will arise and have compassion" (Psalm 102:13 NIV). He cries out in full confidence of God's answer—not because he has anything to offer (he's feeling "destitute"), but because of God's immense love for him. The psalmist's key to enduring suffering is to turn his focus to God's eternal nature, to His promised plan to show mercy to His people.

Endurance in trials comes not from an immediate alleviation of your circumstances but the expectation that you will see the character of the one who holds you fast; that you will see His mercy and favor (see verse 13), His glory—beheld by all the nations of the earth (see verses 15–16); that you will witness those things in your own life as you entrust your life to His care.

Whether you feel destitute—of inspiration, willpower, love, physical strength, holiness—He hears you. He doesn't despise you in your weakness but draws near to you, for nothing can separate you from His love (see Romans 8:38–39). Keep holding on—He will give you strength in the prayer-filled wait for restoration.

FATHER, WHEN I FEEL I HAVE LITTLE TO OFFER,
THANK YOU THAT YOU ALWAYS HEAR MY PRAYER!

Marvelous Love

What marvelous love the Father has extended to us!
Just look at it—we're called children of God!

1 John 3:1 msg

Our world, our culture can become so loud, you may seek a quiet place of peace to escape the noise. As God's child, you have within you His marvelous love, providing a refuge in quiet times with Him.

Think about the cradlesongs that soothe small children when they are nervous, distraught, or fearful. As you sing softly, their tears diminish and a stillness comes over them. Much like a baby's lullaby, God's love can silence worry, confusion, fear, and anxiety in you. His gentle and abiding love flows through you, reminding you that He alone holds the world in His hands.

Charles Finney shared an experience he had of God's amazing love. "The Holy Spirit descended upon me in a manner that seemed to go through me, body and soul. I could feel the impression, like a wave of electricity, going through and through me. Indeed it seemed to come in waves and waves of liquid love. . .like the very breath of God. . . . It seemed to fan me, like immense wings."

Allow God to bring sanctuary to your heart as you take a moment of quiet, resting in His miraculous love.

GOD, POUR YOUR LOVE OUT ON ME AS I TAKE IN THESE QUIET MOMENTS IN YOUR PRESENCE TODAY.

Morning Blessing

"The LORD bless you and keep you; the LORD make his face shine on you and be gracious to you; the LORD turn his face toward you and give you peace."

NUMBERS 6:24–26 NIV

As you head out the door in the morning, remember this blessing given by God to Moses for the Israelites. What wonderful words to begin any journey in your day, be it a commute to work, a drive to the supermarket, a ride to school, or wherever you're heading today. Imagine the joy the Israelites must have felt, to know that God blessed them with a reminder and reassurance of His protection, favor, kindness, approval, and peace.

You too can be confident in God and empowered by all His blessings, such as this one related by God to you through Jeremiah: "For I know the thoughts and plans that I have for you. . .thoughts and plans for welfare and peace and not for evil, to give you hope in your final outcome" (Jeremiah 29:11 AMPC).

Woman of God, the Lord knows your future and gives you peace and hope, even when you cannot see where your life may be heading. What better gift could there be to keep yourself standing tall and unshaken?

DEAR GOD, I THANK YOU FOR THE WONDERFUL BLESSINGS YOU HAVE GIVEN ME. I PRAY YOUR GIFT OF PEACE WOULD BE WITH ME, GIVING ME STRENGTH AND COURAGE TO BEGIN EACH DAY'S JOURNEY.

A Different Cup to Fill

O God, thou art my God; early will I seek thee.

Psalm 63:1 KJV

It is early morning, and we stumble from our beds to take a shower, apply makeup, and blow-dry our hair. Meanwhile, coffee brews in the kitchen, and with a yawn we fill our cups. Busy women have limited time to relax, reflect, and pray. Yet a different and more significant type of cup longs to be filled—our spirits.

King David resided over the nation of Israel and all that that entailed. Yet he found time to seek the counsel, mercy, and direction of God daily. The more responsibilities he assumed, the more he prayed and meditated on God's precepts. Well before David was inundated with worldly concerns, nagging obligations, and his administrative duties, the Bible suggests that he sought the Lord in the early morning hours.

If the king of Israel recognized his need to spend time with God, how much more should we? When we seek our heavenly Father before daily activities demand our attention, the Holy Spirit regenerates our spirits, and our cups overflow.

DEAR LORD, I TAKE THIS TIME TO PRAY AND SPEND TIME WITH YOU BEFORE I ATTEND TO DAILY RESPONSIBILITIES. FILL MY CUP WITH THE PRESENCE AND POWER OF YOUR SPIRIT. GIVE ME THE WISDOM AND DIRECTION I NEED TODAY. AMEN.

Written on Him

"Can a mother forget the baby at her breast and have no compassion on the child she has borne? Though she may forget, I will not forget you!"
ISAIAH 49:15 NIV

God's people during the life of the prophet Isaiah were under threat of captivity, and they saw impending doom. They knew their dark and rebellious hearts brought this about, and they feared that Jehovah would forget or forsake them. God responded by likening Himself to a mother—the ultimate symbol of love and devotion. Mothers care for their children by guiding and protecting them. However, in this fallen world there are also women who abandon their children. God says that unlike weak and broken earthly parents, He will remain steadfast. He can do no less when He says that He engraved His children on the palms of His hands. Carved into His hands! This image comes to life when we consider how Jesus took nails through His hands to save sinners and make them children of God. What a powerful promise: He will never leave us or forsake us.

HOLY GOD, THANK YOU THAT WE CAN CALL YOU ABBA, OR DADDY. THANK YOU THAT JESUS SUFFERED, DIED, AND ROSE AGAIN SO THAT PEOPLE OF ALL TRIBES AND NATIONS COULD KNOW YOU AS FATHER. THANK YOU THAT YOU NEVER FORGET YOUR CHILDREN. HELP US TO NEVER DOUBT YOUR COMPASSION, PROVISION, AND LOVE.

Isolated but Not Alone

"See, I have engraved you on the palms of my hands."
ISAIAH 49:16 NIV

Jesus prayed in the garden of Gethsemane. He knew He stood on the brink of the biggest battle of His earthly life. He craved companionship—support from His friends. He asked His disciples, those closest to Him, to pray, but He discovered them sleeping instead. Then in the night, Judas gave Him away with a kiss. His disciples abandoned Him, friends forgot Him, and Peter, the one who promised to have His back, denied even knowing Him.

As Jesus' captors dragged Him away, He saw no supportive, familiar faces in the crowd. Isolated, He held tight to God. Even when the Father turned away, Jesus called to Him for assurance. Jesus gave up His life and died, fully committed to the Father's plan. He faced death, burial, and resurrection—isolated but not alone. His faith remained unshaken because He knew God would never abandon Him.

No matter what circumstances you are facing today, God has not forgotten you. When you feel isolated, remember that you are never alone.

HEAVENLY FATHER, JUST AS YOU WERE WITH JESUS, I KNOW YOU ARE WITH ME. WHEN OTHERS FORGET ME AND FAIL TO SUPPORT ME, I LOOK TO YOU. YOU ARE MY STRENGTH. YOU ARE ALWAYS WITH ME.

Signs of His Presence

Keep your eyes open for God, watch for his works; be alert for signs of his presence. Remember the world of wonders he has made, his miracles, and the verdicts he's rendered— O seed of Abraham, his servant, O child of Jacob, his chosen.

Psalm 105:4–6 MSG

Life is busy—on purpose! The enemy of your soul wants to keep you preoccupied, filled with any distraction that would keep your eyes off the great works God is doing.

Yet God would have you do otherwise. As writer and pastor Henry Blackaby advises, "Watch to see where God is working and join Him."

Put down your busy schedule and take a deep breath! What's God doing in your life? Perhaps at first glance you saw His fingerprints on your life as coincidence. Look a little closer. Where has He blessed you lately? When has He poured out His favor on you and given you opportunities you otherwise might not have had?

Where's He at work in the lives of your loved ones? How has He intervened? Has someone escaped a car wreck untouched, or not been in the place they planned and so escaped tragedy?

What great work is God doing now, and how can you join Him? When you see Him at work and join Him there, your soul is awake to His presence and in tune with Him.

GOD, OPEN MY EYES TO SEE YOUR WORKS. HELP ME BE WATCHFUL AND RECOGNIZE YOUR PRESENCE.

He's Everywhere

He also asked, "What else is the Kingdom of God like? It is like the yeast a woman used in making bread. Even though she put only a little yeast in three measures of flour, it permeated every part of the dough."

LUKE 13:20–21 NLT

Where is God? Where is His majesty, His miracles, the work of His hands in your life?

God is in the morning sunrise when it's hidden by dewy fog. He's in the oldest evergreen tree in the woods and the budding flower in spring. He's in the comforting touch between spouses, the laughter with friends, and the kindness of strangers.

Jesus says the kingdom of God is in everything you see, touch, and hear. His kingdom is in everything good. Like the yeast in bread, once it's added, it cannot be taken out or seen and counted, but you can see its effects. The dough rises with the help of the yeast, whether it's seen or unseen.

God is like that yeast. He's always working in your life even when you don't see it or feel it. You simply have to trust that His will, His hand, and His way are in the details.

DEAR GOD, I KNOW YOU ARE WITH ME. EVEN WHEN I CAN'T SEE YOU. EVEN WHEN I CAN'T FEEL YOU. I TRUST THAT YOU HAVE GONE AHEAD OF ME AND ARE PLANNING THE WAY AND GUIDING MY STEPS. I TRUST YOU, LORD, TO KNOW WHAT IS BEST. AMEN.

A New Day

God, treat us kindly. You're our only hope. First thing in the morning, be there for us! When things go bad, help us out!

Isaiah 33:2 MSG

There are days that start off wrong and finish worse. Days in which we feel out of sorts, like a tire out of balance, clumsy and inefficient. We say things we shouldn't say, using a voice that is too harsh, too loud. We experience days full of failure, tinged by sin. Wouldn't it be great to redo our bad days?

We have that opportunity. It's called *tomorrow*. Lamentations 3:22–23 tells us that by God's mercies, He gives us a fresh canvas every twenty-four hours. Anger, grudges, irritations, and pain don't have to be a part of it. No matter how stormy the day before, each new day starts fresh. And He is there for us first thing in the morning and every step of the way in our day, even if things begin to go wrong—again.

Every day is a new day, a new beginning, a new chance to enjoy our lives—because each day is a new day with God. We can focus on the things that matter most: worshipping Him, listening to Him, and being in His presence. No matter what happened the day before, we have a fresh start to enjoy a deeper relationship with Him. A fresh canvas, every twenty-four hours.

BEFORE I GET OUT OF BED IN THE MORNING, LET ME SAY THESE WORDS AND MEAN THEM: "THIS IS THE DAY THAT THE LORD HAS MADE; LET US REJOICE AND BE GLAD IN IT" (PSALM 118:24 ESV).

Finding and Sharing Comfort

Praise be to the God and Father of our Lord Jesus Christ, the Father of compassion and the God of all comfort, who comforts us in all our troubles, so that we can comfort those in any trouble with the comfort we ourselves receive from God. For just as we share abundantly in the sufferings of Christ, so also our comfort abounds through Christ.

2 CORINTHIANS 1:3–5 NIV

Young children find comfort in a pacifier or a stuffed animal. Perhaps the most common comfort to them is a special blanket. As you grow older, comfort is harder to find. Certainly, a warm blanket or a hot bubble bath will bring temporary comfort when you are cold. A talk with a friend may soothe your worried heart a bit. But real comfort is found in a relationship with the Lord. No matter what trial or trouble you are facing today, He is there to comfort you. You can rest in Jesus. You can come to Him and lay down your concerns. You can talk with Him, listen to Him, or even just speak His name. There is power and peace to be found in the name of your Savior. One extra benefit to finding comfort in the Lord is that you are then better equipped to comfort others. You can offer a word of compassion to another who is experiencing a similar hurt to that which you have known. You are ready to comfort because you have been comforted.

FATHER, PLEASE COMFORT ME IN THAT AREA OF MY LIFE THAT TROUBLES ME. EQUIP ME TO COMFORT THOSE AROUND ME. AMEN.

Forever Bride

"I will betroth you to me forever; I will betroth you in righteousness and justice, in love and compassion. I will betroth you in faithfulness, and you will acknowledge the LORD."

HOSEA 2:19–20 NIV

Throughout the book of Hosea, God speaks to Israel, His chosen people, who have fallen away and worshipped other gods. They have been unfaithful, breaking the covenant God made with them. The Lord continually compares Israel to a straying wife committing adultery against Him. But despite Israel's rebellion, God still promises to restore her.

These verses may seem distant and irrelevant in the modern world. But as a Christian, you have been adopted into God's nation. You are one of His people, a citizen of His kingdom. When you bow before idols—which can be anything from money to relationships—it grieves the Lord. He is a jealous God, desiring your undivided attention.

But the most astonishing thing is that you are also betrothed to Him to be His bride—beautiful, pure, honored, and cherished. God offers to purify those who enter into a covenant with Him. His wedding gift to you is righteousness, justice, love, compassion, and faithfulness. In all of these things, He never fails or falters.

Rejoice! For you are God's forever-bride.

LORD, YOU ARE THE ULTIMATE LOVER OF MY SOUL. EVEN WHEN I AM UNFAITHFUL, YOU REMAIN FAITHFUL (2 TIMOTHY 2:13). THANK YOU FOR PURSUING ME.

From Death to Life

Paul said, "John's baptism called for repentance from sin. But John himself told the people to believe in the one who would come later, meaning Jesus." As soon as they heard this, they were baptized in the name of the Lord Jesus.

ACTS 19:4–5 NLT

A favorite summer blooming shrub of locals in Tucson, Arizona, the red bird of paradise decorates landscapes with a stunning parade of orange-red flowers, the shrub reaching heights of ten feet or more. The dazzling individual flowers bloom from March to October.

The red bird of paradise has astonishing abilities of recovery, or even what seems to be a rebirth. In the winter, some homeowners cut the shrub back to a foot or so to the ground, leaving the plant looking devastated and completely irrecoverable, only for it to resurrect into flourishing blooms the next summer. In fact, the shrubs can sometimes spring back to life twice the size they were before, as if they died and rose again.

As you surrender your life to Christ, you die to sin and all your old ways, becoming much like a shrub that has been cut back in the winter. Then your new life in Christ brings you up more lovely and beautiful than ever before with the promise of life with Him forever.

HEAVENLY FATHER, THANK YOU FOR THE GIFT OF SAVING ME FROM DEATH AND GIVING ME ETERNAL LIFE.

Praise and Seek

Honor his holy name with Hallelujahs, you who seek God. Live a happy life! Keep your eyes open for God, watch for his works; be alert for signs of his presence. Remember the world of wonders he has made, his miracles, and the verdicts he's rendered.

Psalm 105:3–5 MSG

When worries are overloading you, when you feel you cannot catch a breath, when you wonder where God has gone, don't hide under the covers. Instead, honor God. Praise His name. Shout out hallelujahs. And seek the one who holds your life and breath in His hands.

For when you seek God, you will find Him. That's a vow God makes repeatedly, such as in Deuteronomy 4:29: "If. . .you will seek (inquire for and require as necessity) the Lord your God, you will find Him if you [truly] seek Him with all your heart [and mind] and soul and life" (AMPC).

"Seeking" doesn't mean a quick morning glance at the Bible or a short hum of a hymn. This is an all-in kind of seeking, a looking for Him with *all* your heart, mind, soul, and life.

And once you start seeking Him, keep your eyes open for where He's working. Watch carefully for signs of His presence. Stay aware of all the wonders He's performed, the promises He's kept, the judgments He's made.

Today, praise and seek your God. And all His power, strength, and wonders will uphold you.

LORD, I COME WITH OPEN EYES,
SEEKING YOU WITH ALL I AM.

The Guardian of Your Life

May Your mercy come to me. . .for my soul is safe within You,
the guardian of my life. I will seek protection in the shade
of Your wings until the destruction has passed. I cry out to
God, the Most High, . . .who always does what is good for me.
Out of heaven my rescue comes. He dispatches His mercy
and truth and goes after whoever tries to run over me.

PSALM 57:1–3 VOICE

What if you woke up every morning with the assurance that a heavenly guardian was watching over you? And this divine protector offered you safety, goodness, mercy, truth, and more? How might that change your attitude and outlook for the day? Would you be more optimistic? Would your worries take a backseat to your hopes and dreams? Would you have an extra spring in your step?

If so, friend, then you'll be glad to know this isn't some far-fetched fantasy—it's your marvelous reality! Just as David relied on the mercy and protection of God while he was being pursued by his enemies, you can rely on the heavenly Father too. In the best of times or—most importantly—in the worst of times, the Most High will rescue you and keep you safe from harm. Ask Him to wrap you in His loving protection today.

GUARDIAN OF MY LIFE, I PRAISE YOU—MY RESCUER, MY SAVIOR, MY FRIEND, AND MY LOYAL PROTECTOR.

God's Grace in Weakness

"My grace is all you need. My power works best in weakness." So now I am glad to boast about my weaknesses, so that the power of Christ can work through me. That's why I take pleasure in my weaknesses, and in the insults, hardships, persecutions, and troubles that I suffer for Christ. For when I am weak, then I am strong.

2 Corinthians 12:9–10 NLT

The apostle Paul had many amazing experiences over the years after his conversion, and he saw God bring him through many experiences, each designed to draw him ever closer to his goal to be like Christ. One such experience was getting to visit heaven, whether in the spirit or out of the spirit—either in reality or in a vision—he didn't know. But in order to keep Paul humble, the Lord sent a "thorn in the flesh."

Scripture doesn't say exactly what that "thorn" was, but it caused Paul enough pain and trouble that he asked the Lord to take it away, not once but three times. Finally God told him, "My grace is all you need. My power works best in weakness." In other words, "No. All you need is My grace to help you cope with this thorn. For in your weakness you are forced to depend on Me for strength to get you through and still be able to proclaim My gospel. Others can see Me in you, when your 'thorn' should keep you from doing anything at all."

FATHER, HELP ME TO RELY ON YOUR GRACE AS PAUL DID, KNOWING YOU ALLOW WEAKNESS TO KEEP ME FROM WORKING INDEPENDENTLY.

Even Now

"Even now," declares the Lord, *"return to me with all your heart, with fasting and weeping and mourning." Rend your heart and not your garments. Return to the* Lord *your God, for he is gracious and compassionate, slow to anger and abounding in love, and he relents from sending calamity.*

Joel 2:12–13 niv

The Israelites had periods of great rebellion against God. They turned to terrible pagan idols made of wood and stone. They ignored God's laws and no longer relied on Him. They forgot they were God's treasured possession, holy among the nations.

Like Israel, you have probably rebelled against the Lord at some point in your life. You have strayed far from home. And when you look over your shoulder to see how far you have gone, you tell yourself that it's too late to turn back. You have done too much. Wandered too far. Surely if you went home, God's gates would be firmly shut, barring your reentrance.

But God says, "*Even now* return to me." Even after all you have done—after all the idols you have pursued, and all the commandments you have broken—come back home. All He requires is your whole heart, brimming with repentance. A heart that has been torn by the remembrance of the depth of your depravity and your deep, deep need for a Savior.

Like Israel, you also are God's treasured possession, His precious child. His gates remain open, anticipating your return.

LORD, TRULY YOU ARE GRACIOUS AND COMPASSIONATE, ABOUNDING IN LOVE. THANK YOU.

Private Audience

Thus Solomon finished the house of the LORD and the king's house; and Solomon successfully accomplished all that came into his heart to make in the house of the LORD and in his own house. Then the LORD appeared to Solomon by night, and said to him: "I have heard your prayer, and have chosen this place for Myself as a house of sacrifice."

2 CHRONICLES 7:11–12 NKJV

You've no doubt experienced someone being distracted while you're trying to have a conversation with her. That person may drift off in her own mind, get a phone call, or hear the annoying bleep of an incoming text message or the tiny voice of a child calling her name.

Your human audience may lose its attention, but your heavenly one won't. Father God is always listening. His eyes are ever on you, never looking above your head to see who's walked into the room. He gives you a private audience any time you want to talk with Him. You're His focus, and He values every moment you give Him.

Even when you feel you're alone, you can trust God's there. He's an audience that never leaves the auditorium of your life. When you speak, He hears every word. And as you return the favor by listening to Him, He'll lead you, guide you, and show you things you'd never discover on your own.

HEAVENLY FATHER, THANK YOU FOR LISTENING TO ME. SHOW ME THE PLANS YOU HAVE FOR MY LIFE.

Wait for the Morning

I wait for the Lord more than watchmen wait for the morning, more than watchmen wait for the morning.

Psalm 130:6 niv

Watchmen were guards who stood on the walls of ancient cities to look out for enemies. These men would sound an alarm if they saw danger approaching. This alert allowed the men of the city to prepare to protect their families.

As a watchman, it was important to stay awake during the night hours. But this was more than difficult. For the night was dark with no city lights to help the watchman see off into the distance. Torch light only traveled so far. Not only was it difficult to see, but the hours seemed so long without anything to help pass the time. The watchmen were never sure what might happen in those pitch-black nights.

Many women today may feel like those watchmen of ancient days. Life may seem dark, long, and unpredictable. But just as the watchmen waited for the first rays of sunshine to come over the horizon, God's daughters must wait to see their Father working.

The watchmen trusted that morning would come. And it always did. Just as it will for you. For God always works and reveals Himself to His beloved at just the right time.

LORD, WHEN I'M IN A DARK PLACE, I PROMISE TO WAIT FOR YOUR GUIDANCE MORE THAN WATCHMEN WAIT FOR THE MORNING, MORE THAN WATCHMEN WAIT FOR THE MORNING.

Wish List

But they cried the more, saying, Have mercy on us, O Lord, thou son of David. And Jesus stood still, and called them, and said, What will ye that I shall do unto you?

MATTHEW 20:31–32 KJV

The two blind men heard that Jesus was passing by. They called out a generic plea: "Have mercy on us!"

The man they addressed as "Lord" and "son of David" stopped in His tracks. He responded with a simple question: "What do you want?"

Wasn't it obvious? Jesus knew their thoughts and what their hearts desired. But that wasn't enough. They had to verbalize their request: "We want our *sight*"—the one thing they could not receive without divine intervention. Jesus answered their prayer by opening their eyes—and they responded by following Him.

God wants us to bring specific needs to Him. Do you need a job? Tell Him how much salary you need, what kind of work you like to do, and where you want to commute. Do you need a new home? Tell Him exactly what you'd like.

God doesn't *need* us to tell Him our desires. He already knows them. But He delights in going above and beyond what we can ask for. He loves to demonstrate His lavish love. Even if He doesn't appear to give us what we want, it's because He has something better in store.

God wants us to bring the wishes of our hearts to Him in prayer.

HEAVENLY FATHER, I THANK YOU THAT YOU CARE ABOUT THE SMALLEST DETAILS OF MY LIFE. TEACH ME THE JOY OF SPECIFIC PRAYER.

G.R.A.C.E.

Because he was full of grace and truth,
from him we all received one gift after another.
JOHN 1:16 NCV

Perhaps you've seen the acronym for G.R.A.C.E. (God's Riches at Christ's Expense). What does that mean for us, His daughters? We face all sorts of challenges and sometimes feel depleted and dry. In those moments, all of God's riches (peace, joy, long-suffering, favor, help) are ours. What did we do to deserve them? Nothing. That's the point of grace: Someone else paid the price so that we could receive God's gifts for free.

Take a good look at today's scripture. God promises not only to give grace and truth, but "one gift after another." Picture yourself as a little girl at your daddy's knee. Now picture him giving you not one gift. . .not two. . .but one on top of the other, on top of the other. He overwhelms you with his beautifully wrapped gifts, topped off with ribbons and bows. Talk about blowing your socks off!

God does the same thing when He "gifts" us with things we don't deserve: forgiveness, comfort, satisfaction, provision. What a generous God we serve!

FATHER, I KNOW THAT I HAVEN'T DONE ANYTHING TO DESERVE YOUR GRACE. . .YOUR GIFTS. AND YET, YOU CONTINUE TO POUR THESE THINGS OUT ON MY LIFE ANYWAY. THANK YOU FOR YOUR GRACE, LORD. YOU GIVE, AND GIVE, AND THEN GIVE SOME MORE.

Unity with the Father

"Love your enemies and pray for those who persecute you, that you may be children of your Father in heaven. . . . Be perfect, therefore, as your heavenly Father is perfect."

MATTHEW 5:44–45, 48 NIV

The biggest challenge facing you today is probably a person—what she said or did—or didn't say or do—to you or someone you love. Relationships are difficult on any level—from someone you have never met who takes *your* parking place, to your closest friend who makes a disparaging remark about you, to your perfect prince who acts like a frog.

It's easy to get caught up in the drama when someone pushes your buttons or you feel used, abandoned, mistreated, or hurt. Society is full of people looking for revenge and a way to make someone pay for the wrongs done to them. As a child of God, you can choose another way—your heavenly Father's way.

He responds with grace and forgiveness to both good and evil people. He is the calm in the middle of the storm. He desires to put His love, poured out lavishly upon you, to work *in* you and let it operate *through* you. You can rest in His peace, knowing He chose a perfect way for you.

FATHER, THANK YOU FOR POURING YOUR LOVE OUT ON ME. I DESIRE TO WALK IN UNITY WITH YOU, ALLOWING YOUR LOVE TO FLOW THROUGH ME AND RESPONDING IN PEACE TO ALL.

Whatever Seems Good

Then the king said to Zadok, "Take the ark of God back into the city. If I find favor in the LORD's eyes, he will bring me back and let me see it and his dwelling place again. But if he says, 'I am not pleased with you,' then I am ready; let him do to me whatever seems good to him."

2 SAMUEL 15:25–26 NIV

King David was in dire straits. The hearts of his people had been won by his son and usurper, Absalom. So David had to flee Jerusalem. The people in the countryside cried as the king and his retinue passed by. Even the Levites had followed him with the ark of God. But David told the priest Zadok to go back to the city with the ark. Not knowing what was going to happen, David determined to leave his life in the hands of God, ready for whatever would happen, satisfied God would do what He deemed best. This sentiment is echoed later by Jesus who would one day, while in a Jerusalem garden, pray to Father God, "Not My will but Yours."

When all looks hopeless, when your dreams have become nightmares, how wonderful to be calm and content, rather than complaining. Have no fear of whatever the future may hold, knowing all events are in God's hands.

WHATEVER YOU WISH AND WILL, LORD, I'M READY. I AND MY LIFE ARE IN YOUR HANDS, KNOWING YOU KNOW BEST.

The Greatest

"But I tell you, in this you are not right,
for God is greater than any mortal."
JOB 33:12 NIV

Everyone experiences a bad day every once in a while. You know the kind, a day when you wish you'd never gotten out of bed in the morning. Imagine if that one day turned into another. . .and another. . .and another. . .and each day worse than the last. Ultimately you'd be brought to your knees, unable to fathom what brought you to this place. That's the well-known story of Job.

Job lost everything—his livelihood, his children, his health—and did what most people would do: He tried to figure out why. Three of Job's friends offered suggestions for the cause of his misery, adding fuel to his despondency. It took a young man, Elihu, who finally offered wisdom. Job was trying to use the logic of man to rationalize a matter of God. A mere mortal could never understand God's plan. But by keeping the faith, ultimately, a person will be blessed.

Why do bad things happen to good people? We may never understand why this happens. But by keeping the faith, as Job did, God will always bring you through. Remember that the next time you have a bad day. If God brings you to it, He'll bring you through it.

DEAR GOD, ON MY DARKEST DAYS,
HELP ME TO REMEMBER THAT YOU HAVE
EVERYTHING UNDER CONTROL AND WILL SEE
ME THROUGH THE GOOD AND BAD TIMES.

A Child in Need

"For all those things My hand has made, and all those things exist," says the LORD. *"But on this one will I look: on him who is poor and of a contrite spirit, and who trembles at My word."*

ISAIAH 66:2 NKJV

When a teacher looks across a room full of students working quietly at their desks, which one gets her attention? The one with a raised hand—the one with an immediate need.

Like the student, a humble child of God with a need catches His eye. Though He is always watching over all of us, He is drawn to a child who needs Him. We may need forgiveness, wisdom, courage, endurance, patience, health, protection, or even a reassurance of His love. God promises to come to our aid when He sees us with a hand up, reaching for His assistance. He will not ignore a contrite heart and spirit. God's grace rushes to the one who cries out for mercy, and He offers restoration to the repentant heart.

What needs do you have in your life today? Raise your hand in prayer to God. He'll take care of your needs and then some—blessing your life in ways you can't even imagine!

FATHER, THANK YOU FOR CARING ABOUT THE NEEDS OF YOUR CHILDREN. HELP ME TO REMEMBER TO ALWAYS SEEK YOU FIRST.

Whiter than Snow

Take away my sin, and I will be clean.
Wash me, and I will be whiter than snow.
PSALM 51:7 NCV

If you've ever looked out over a pristine field covered in glistening mounds of white snow, you know what purity looks like. Everything underneath those mounds of snow has disappeared from view, to be seen no more. The white snow covers it all, making it irrelevant.

That's how forgiveness works. When we come to God and confess our sins, He is faithful and just to forgive us (see 1 John 1:91). His forgiveness washes over us in exactly the same way that the snow covers the ground below. All traces of yesterday—the awful things we've done, the pain we've caused, the heartache we've gone through—are gone. In place of the bad memories is glistening white forgiveness, sparkling with the hope of better days to come.

If you haven't yet asked Jesus to be the Lord of your life, if you haven't accepted His forgiveness for the sins you've committed, this is the perfect day—the perfect season—to do so. He can wash your sins away and leave you whiter than snow.

FATHER, EVEN WHEN IT'S SPRINGTIME, I LOVE THE IMAGE OF SNOW THAT I FIND IN THIS SCRIPTURE. IT'S A REMINDER THAT MY PAST REALLY CAN BE IN THE PAST. I WANT TO LIVE FOR TODAY, LORD, SO THAT I CAN HAVE THE COURAGE TO STEP INTO TOMORROW WITHOUT WORRYING ABOUT WHAT HAPPENED YESTERDAY. CLEANSE ME, LORD!

Grace Given

So the last shall be first, and the first last:
for many be called, but few chosen.
MATTHEW 20:16 KJV

Is receiving grace a hard concept for you to accept from God? Often it may be easier to extend grace to another person as opposed to extending it to yourself or receiving grace from another.

You might follow all of the commandments (see Exodus 20:3–17) or sing praises to the Lord (see Psalm 30), but you still feel like something isn't right between you and God. Could it be that something is holding you captive and enslaving you to the point where there is a figurative barrier between you and God?

The parable of the workers in the vineyard, found in Matthew 20:1–16, is about God's grace in your life. Sometimes it doesn't feel fair when grace is given to others. You might want justice. And when the tables are turned, it may be hard for you also to receive unmerited favor.

Why some people are given their fair share, others less, and some more doesn't always seem to make sense. What is clear is that God loves you no matter what! Even when circumstances in your life don't make sense, abide in Him. As you do, watch the barricade in your life come tumbling down because you are open to the grace He gives.

LORD JESUS, I COME TO YOU WITH THE DESIRE TO PLACE YOU FIRST IN MY LIFE. I CHOOSE TO RECEIVE YOUR GRACE AND EXTEND IT TO OTHERS.

Blessed Believer

That Sunday evening the disciples were meeting behind locked doors because they were afraid. . . . Suddenly, Jesus was standing there among them! "Peace be with you," he said. . . . Eight days later the disciples were together again, and this time Thomas was with them. The doors were locked; but suddenly, as before, Jesus was standing among them. "Peace be with you," he said.

John 20:19, 26 NLT

No matter where you are, Jesus can reach you. No matter what barriers, locked doors, or walls are surrounding you, Jesus can get through, stand beside you, show you His face, His hands, His feet, His love, His Spirit. No doors can shut out His presence.

And where Jesus gains entrance, His peace follows. He blesses you with peace with God, with your own conscience, and with others. His presence stills the storms of your life, the waves of anxiety, the eddies of troubles. He not only gives you His peace but asks you to carry it with you.

Although you have not yet met Jesus physically face-to-face, nor put your hands on His wounds, Jesus favors you because of your trust in Him. He said, "Blessed and happy and to be envied are those who have never seen Me and yet have believed and adhered to and trusted and relied on Me" (John 20:29 AMPC).

"Peace be with you."

LORD, NOTHING CAN KEEP YOU FROM ME! THANK YOU FOR THE CALMING PEACE YOUR PRESENCE PROVIDES.

The Living God

"I decree that everyone throughout my kingdom should tremble with fear before the God of Daniel. For he is the living God, and he will endure forever. His kingdom will never be destroyed, and his rule will never end. He rescues and saves his people; he performs miraculous signs and wonders in the heavens and on earth. He has rescued Daniel from the power of the lions."

DANIEL 6:26–27 NLT

King Darius made a decree that for thirty days, no one in his kingdom could pray to anyone or anything other than himself. But Daniel, who trusted God with his life, decided to keep praying to God just as he always had. When his disobedience was discovered, Daniel was tossed into a den of hungry lions.

Imagine Darius' amazement the next morning when he found Daniel alive and well—without a single scratch from the lions. This unbelievable miracle caused Darius to have a complete change of heart. And so he made a proclamation that everyone in his kingdom should fear Daniel's God—Darius knew there was no power like the power of the living God.

How wonderful that Daniel's God is still our God today. He still rescues. He still saves. He still performs miracles. He is King forever!

MIRACLE WORKER, MY KING, THANK YOU FOR BEING THE SAME GOD TODAY THAT YOU HAVE BEEN SINCE THE BEGINNING OF TIME. YOUR UNWAVERING LOVE, YOUR PROMISE KEEPING, HELP TO CREATE AN UNSHAKABLE FAITH IN ME! AMEN.

Persistently Presented Petitions

"O woman, great is your faith! Let it be to you as you desire."
Matthew 15:28 NKJV

When our loved ones are troubled, our hearts are heavy and we feel helpless. But with Christ's ear within reach of our voices, we are anything but powerless. We have an interceder, someone to whom we can continually go and present our petitions.

In Matthew 15:21–28, a Canaanite woman asked Jesus for mercy and to heal her demon-possessed daughter. At first Christ seemed not to hear her pleas. The disciples, irritated with her persistence, told Jesus to send her away.

Yet this woman had dogged determination. She *knew* that the Son of God could heal her daughter. She continued to plead, driven by love for her child and faith in Christ's power.

Her insistence was met by a reproach from Christ, who told her He did not come to help the Gentiles but the Jews. This had to have crushed her expectations. Yet even then she persisted. She did not despair but continued running after Him, worshipping Him, pleading with Him, begging for mercy.

Jesus reproached her again. But still she was undeterred. Finally, Jesus said the words we all long to hear: "Woman, great is your faith! Let it be to you as you desire."

May we live our lives as persistent in our petitions as the Canaanite woman. And may God see our faith and honor our requests as we boldly bring the needs of others before His throne!

GOD, I COME TO YOU, BRINGING THE CONCERNS OF OTHERS. LORD, HAVE MERCY! AMEN.

Cleaning Up

Come close to God and He will come close to you. [Recognize that you are] sinners, get your soiled hands clean. . .and purify your hearts.

James 4:8 AMPC

Picture a muddy, unshorn sheep. A shepherd would have a job before him to clean up that animal because the fleece is quite deep. He must dig down with the shears layer by layer, tugging at the wool as he goes. In order to shear the sheep, he has to have hold of it, a firm grasp on a wiggling, uncooperative animal. Whatever it takes, the shepherd must clean the sheep.

Now picture us. Uncooperative, squirming, with insides that need to be cleaned. Our thoughts and actions have not been pure. Maybe we have lost our tempers, taken advantage of another, or gossiped. Actions which are not what God wants of us. Actions that are called sin. Sin which blackens the heart. Like the sheep, we must be gathered in and cleaned.

Our most glorious God has promised He will do that for us when we ask. If we draw near to God and ask for His forgiveness, He will cleanse our hearts and make us a part of His fold. Hallelujah. What a magnificent and overwhelming plan He has for us!

DEAR LORD, IS GAINING A NEW LIFE TRULY AS SIMPLE AS THAT? I REACH OUT MY HAND IN SURRENDER AND ASK YOU TO BECOME THE KING OF MY LIFE. THANK YOU FOR ALL YOU HAVE DONE FOR ME. AMEN.

Poured Out

Then the LORD said to Moses, "Give the following instructions to the people of Israel. This is how you are to deal with those who sin unintentionally by doing anything that violates one of the LORD's commands."

LEVITICUS 4:1–2 NLT

The words to describe the book of Leviticus present an oxymoron, for it is both mundane and marvelous. It's a book about worship, obedience, and being set apart by God as holy. It's also a firsthand glimpse of what life was like for sinful people who had to adhere to very strict laws.

But in Matthew 26, you read how Jesus is betrayed and then goes before Pilate. How He's sentenced to crucifixion, a punishment He didn't deserve but endured on your behalf anyway, so that your sins would be forgiven and you could be reconciled to God. What Jesus did on the cross finished what was required in Leviticus. The strict law ended as grace, love, mercy, and forgiveness poured out.

Abiding in Jesus allows for reflection on what was and now is in your life. How strict are you being with yourself and others? Where do you wish you were more gracious, loving, merciful, and forgiving? Ask God to help you take inventory today.

JESUS, I NEED YOUR GRACE TO BE KIND, LOVING, AND COMPASSIONATE TOWARD MYSELF AND OTHERS. THANK YOU FOR THE FREEDOM TO WALK IN YOUR LOVE AND GRACE.

One Judge

Search me [thoroughly], O God, and know my heart! Try me and know my thoughts! And see if there is any wicked or hurtful way in me, and lead me in the way everlasting.

PSALM 139:23–24 AMPC

Your heart is as complex and difficult to understand as a puzzle with a vast number of unique pieces. It contains strong desires, fears, pride, love, tenderness, anger, sadness, and more. Who can possibly comprehend its true content? The answer is God. He can discern the innermost parts of your heart and help you better understand your own thoughts, feelings, and actions.

Seek God's perspective on the contents of your heart. Trust His kind and thorough judgments. Ask God where corrections need to be made. Is there pride lurking behind a broken relationship? Are sharp fragments of jealousy tearing at your joy?

God's desire is for you to be free from the tight, constraining grasp of sin's chokehold. He wants you to be free to experience all the confidence, peace, and joy you were created for in life. Take His hand and let Him lead you through the process of redeeming your heart and mind as only He can.

GOD, PLEASE SEARCH MY HEART AND MIND AND SHOW ME WHAT YOU WANT TO CHANGE IN ME. I TRUST YOU TO BREAK ME FREE OF OLD THOUGHT PATTERNS AND FEELINGS. LEAD ME IN YOUR NEW WAY.

Shining Strength

Turn us again, O God, and cause thy face
to shine; and we shall be saved.
PSALM 80:3 KJV

On an overcast day, our energy can be at a low ebb. It feels dark and limp, even with bright lights in the home or office. Of course, we all like a rainy day now and then, but it does seem to fit better with huddling under a quilt than with tackling energetic projects. But notice the difference to your mood when the clouds start to split and a ray of sunshine beams through.

In school we learned that the sun is always shining just above the clouds. But that doesn't seem possible when all we can see is the dark, menacing atmosphere around us. Yet then when the sun starts to dance and glitter in happy rays, there is suddenly a lift to everything.

In scripture, the imagery of God causing His face to shine on someone is symbolic of His blessing. The psalmist acknowledges that the only way Israel will be saved from her calamities and her transgressions is for the mercies of God to shine down on her.

Are you under a spiritual cloud today?

Does it seem that all is dark?

Do you need mercy for sin or grace for trials?

Remember God is above all.

Turn to Him and ask Him to turn His face to you. He will. He promised.

GOD, TODAY PLEASE TURN YOUR FACE TO ME AND SHINE DOWN GRACE FOR MY NEED. AMEN.

Known by God

But if anyone loves God, he is known by God.
1 CORINTHIANS 8:3 ESV

How do we show that we love God? Is it by church attendance? Giving? Doing good deeds? Prayer? These may be manifestations of our love for God, or they may be things we do out of a sense of duty; but loving God is first and foremost a response to being known and loved by God. We can't muster emotion or feeling toward God nor do we love Him simply by willing ourselves to acts of obedience. We begin to love God when we grasp what it means to be known by God.

He knit us together in our mothers' wombs.

He knows the number of hairs on our heads.

He knows every quirk of our personalites and gave us every talent that we have.

He accepts us as we are because of Christ's sacrifice for us.

He has compassion for our weakness.

He forgives our sins.

He longs to commune with us.

He delights to hear our prayers.

He desires to help us, strengthen us, and bless us.

He has given us the Holy Spirit as our comforter, our helper, and our teacher.

We need to reacquaint ourselves with the gospel often, to meditate on what Christ has done for us, and to remember that He first loved us.

LORD, RENEW MY LOVE FOR YOU.

I Am

God said to Moses, "I AM WHO I AM. This is what you are to say to the Israelites: 'I AM has sent me to you.'"
EXODUS 3:14 NIV

The words "I am" ring out in the present tense. These words are used some seven hundred times in the Bible to describe God and Jesus. When Moses was on the mount and asked God who He was, a voice thundered, "I Am." In the New Testament, Jesus said of Himself, "I am the bread of life; I am the light of the world; I am the good shepherd; I am the way; I am the resurrection." Present tense. Words of hope and life. I Am.

Who is God to you today? Is He in the present tense? Living, loving, presiding over your life? Is the Lord of lords "I Was" or "I've Never Been" to you? Have you experienced the hope which comes from an everlasting "I Am" Father? One who walks by you daily and will never let go? "I Am with you always."

We are surprised when we struggle in the world, yet we hesitate to turn to our very Creator. He has the answers, and He will fill us with hope. Reach for Him today. Don't be uncertain. Know Him. For He is, after all, I Am.

FATHER, I SURRENDER MY LIFE TO YOU THIS DAY. I CHOOSE TO TURN FROM MY SINS, REACH FOR YOUR HAND, AND ASK FOR YOUR GUIDANCE. THANK YOU FOR YOUR LOVING-KINDNESS. AMEN.

By His Grace

Praise the Lord, the God of Israel, who lives from everlasting to everlasting. Amen and amen!
Psalm 41:13 NLT

Praising God in all seasons is a tough thing to do. When circumstances aren't good, you might be tempted to blame God more than praise Him. And when circumstances are great, you might be tempted to believe you did something right to deserve all of the blessings and favor being showered on you.

What is the truth? God wants you to praise Him in good times and in bad. It's when you praise Him during the hard times that He increases your faith and helps you to see His goodness in all situations. When you praise Him in the good times, you fully appreciate all that He has done in and through you, only by His grace.

As you focus on abiding in Christ, think of five things you are grateful for today. Write them down in your journal or on a sticky note. Throughout the day, look at your list and praise Him for those things. If you can think of more than five—great! Remember the giver of grace, and how it's only *by* His grace that you have been saved and freed up to praise Him.

JESUS, THANK YOU FOR EVERYTHING YOU HAVE DONE AND GIVEN ME! THANK YOU THAT THIS LIFE ISN'T ABOUT MY WORKS. IT'S ALL ABOUT YOUR GRACE. THANK YOU FOR YOUR ENDLESS SUPPLY OF BLESSINGS.

Faithful in Our Longing

Soon afterward his wife, Elizabeth, became pregnant and went into seclusion for five months. "How kind the Lord is!" she exclaimed. "He has taken away my disgrace of having no children."

LUKE 1:24–25 NLT

For her and Zechariah's whole marriage, Elizabeth had been barren. Her culture deemed childlessness a disgrace, for the Lord opening the womb was a sign of blessing on the Israelites' obedience (see Leviticus 26:3, 9). No doubt the couple—who're described as "righteous in God's eyes" (Luke 1:6 NLT)—wondered why God hadn't given them children. Despite that, they continued serving faithfully into their later years.

Notice Elizabeth's response after she becomes miraculously pregnant: "How kind the Lord is!" There's no anger or resentment in her words—just praising God for His kindness in fulfilling her heart's desire. And He gave her the honor of bearing the one who would point the way to the Messiah.

Maybe you also have longings you've been praying about for years; maybe thinking of continuing faithfully, as Elizabeth did, feels too hard to bear. But you're loved. Your heavenly Father sees you and keeps track of all your tears (see Psalm 56:8). He'll remain faithfully by your side, to comfort and bind up your broken heart (see Psalm 147:3). Keep seeking His goodness, for you will find it; He'll give you strength to go on.

LORD, WHETHER YOU FULFILL MY LONGING OR NOT, KEEP ON SHOWING ME THAT YOU ARE MY GREAT REWARD (GENESIS 15:1).

Remembering the Promise Keeper

"As my life was slipping away, I remembered the LORD*. And my earnest prayer went out to you in your holy Temple. Those who worship false gods turn their backs on all God's mercies. But I will offer sacrifices to you with songs of praise, and I will fulfill all my vows. For my salvation comes from the* LORD *alone."*

JONAH 2:7–9 NLT

Jonah, likely overwhelmed by sorrow, had all but given up hope on life. He had made some not-so-great decisions and had tried to run away from God. . .and he now was feeling the full weight of his sinful and shortsighted consequences.

And yet. . .Jonah "remembered." Although his remembering of the Lord appears to be quite late, remember God he did. He remembered God was the ultimate promise keeper. He remembered God was gracious and full of mercy. He remembered God was healer and forgiver and Savior. And after his prayer to God, Jonah received Christ's blessing.

No matter what mistakes you've made, know this: There is beauty in your remembering who God is. And while we might treat God badly for a time or even try to run away from Him, He is *always* waiting and ready for us to seek Him again. Still, He cares. Still, He loves.

HEAVENLY FATHER, I'M SORRY FOR EVER TRYING TO RUN AWAY FROM YOU. I NEED YOU—TODAY AND EVERY DAY. PLEASE KEEP MY THOUGHTS FOCUSED ON YOU AND YOUR STEADFAST GOODNESS AND MERCY.

The New Me

Therefore, if anyone is in Christ, the new creation has come: The old has gone, the new is here!
2 CORINTHIANS 5:17 NIV

Are you in Christ? Is He consistently Lord of your life? Then you are a new creation.

Regardless of your past, regardless of the circumstances you may have faced, you're a new creation. All the past guilt is gone—vanished, obliterated—and everything is new.

It's true that some of us live with the consequences of past choices. Maybe our children are the result of premarital sex—but they are nonetheless marvelous miracles of God. Maybe today's health problems result from years of unwise and harmful choices—but God says the guilt is all in the past, gone. Everything is new. What's history is done and over—and Jesus has replaced our old with His new: new peace, new joy, new love, new strength.

Since God Himself sees us as a new creation, how can we do any less? We need to choose to see ourselves as a new creation too. And we can, through God's grace.

If you are "in Christ," you are a new creation. Be glad. Give thanks. Live each day as the new creation you have become through Jesus.

FATHER, I'M SO THANKFUL THAT YOU ARE A GOD OF GRACE—AND I THANK YOU THAT I AM A NEW CREATION. PLEASE GIVE ME THE SPIRITUAL EYES TO SEE MYSELF AS A NEW CREATION, LOOKING PAST THE GUILT OF YESTERDAY'S CHOICES.

With a Song on His Lips

"The Lord *your God is with you, the Mighty Warrior who saves. He will take great delight in you. . . [He] will rejoice over you with singing."*
Zephaniah 3:17 NIV

Our relationships with our earthly fathers can greatly affect how we view our heavenly Father. Whether consciously or not, we take the earthly father we can see and try to puzzle out what our heavenly Father is like. Some women had attentive, loving fathers. If only this were the norm! Some fathers were absent, never known to their daughters. Other fathers violated the family's trust through abuse or neglect. Some fathers were caring but distant—their emotional connection difficult or non-existent.

Where our earthly fathers have fallen short, our heavenly Father does all perfectly and to the full. He is full of mercy, full of loving-kindness, absolutely just and right. He brings order where there is disorder, peace instead of confusion. He heals bodies and broken hearts, and He keeps all His promises.

Though the Father rules over the whole universe, He is also close to us. He does not love us at arm's length, His disapproval looming if we misstep. He *sings* and *rejoices* over His children; He *delights* in that we belong to Him. The love of our great God surpasses all earthly love in its perfection, its sacrifice, its provision, and its salvation. Regardless of our family backgrounds, our Creator perfectly loves and delights in us.

FATHER GOD, THANK YOU FOR MAKING ME YOUR DAUGHTER.

Constant Help

Lord, I believe! [Constantly] help my weakness of faith!
MARK 9:24 AMPC

A man's young son had issues. He would go into convulsions, foam at the mouth, grind his teeth, and then fall into a stupor. The danger was that the boy would be thrown into fire and water. The loving yet desperate father said to Jesus, "If You can do anything, do have pity on us and help us" (Mark 9:22 AMPC).

Jesus replied, "[You say to Me], If You can do anything? [Why,] all things can be (are possible) to him who believes!" (Mark 9:23 AMPC). That's when the father asked Jesus to constantly help him with his weakness of faith. Moments later, Jesus healed the boy of his affliction.

Jesus has one request when you ask for help with your own issues: Take the *if* out of the equation when it comes to believing in His power. Have faith that *He can do anything* in your life, that for Him *nothing is impossible*.

But if (and *when*) you do fall short in faith, know that the Lord will constantly help you, pouring on you more than a sufficient amount of grace, enabling Him to work even through your weakness.

No matter what your level of faith, constantly call on Jesus. He will come, grip your hand, and lift you up into a life of seemingly impossible miracles.

JESUS, EVERYTHING IS POSSIBLE WITH YOU IN MY HEART. HELP ME TO BELIEVE THIS MORE AND MORE EACH DAY.

You Are Loved

Love is patient, love is kind. It does not envy, it does not boast, it is not proud. It does not dishonor others, it is not self-seeking, it is not easily angered, it keeps no record of wrongs. Love does not delight in evil but rejoices with the truth.

1 Corinthians 13:4–6 NIV

We may not have great success at implementing this impressive list of love's qualities. God, however, never fails at loving us completely and enduringly. All our lives, He has loved us with patience and kindness. And although the people around us may also fail to meet God's high standard of love, He does not. He is never irritable or resentful with us, and He rejoices over us when we make good choices.

Understanding how God sees us is critical to our trusting Him. Sometimes our brains tell us that we're trusting when our emotions are still fearful. That's because head knowledge is different from heart knowledge. It's when our hearts are satisfied and assured that His affection doesn't waver that we can trust God completely.

Take a deep breath and relax in the truth that God is good and you can trust Him with every part of your life: your family, work, relationships, health, and more. Look back over your life and remember the ways God has proven His great love for you. Rest in His affection today.

GOD, THANK YOU FOR YOUR PERFECT LOVE.
HELP ME TO LET GO OF FEAR AND TRUST YOU.

Unchanging, Constant

"I am God—yes, I Am. I haven't changed."
Malachi 3:6 MSG

In our human relationships, it's virtually impossible to find a person who will never let us down. . .someone who follows through on every single promise. . .someone who always shows up. . .someone who loves us on our good days and our "difficult to love" days. No human being is perfect—including us. And imperfect people make for imperfect relationships.

In a world of all this imperfection, what a relief to know that we can have a beautifully secure relationship with the Father! He is steadfast and true to His Word. We never need to wonder where He stands or how He feels about us, because He is unchanging.

When you're feeling unsure, wrap your soul in these comforting scriptures:

- Hebrews 13:8
- James 1:17
- Numbers 23:19
- Isaiah 40:8
- Psalm 119:89
- Psalm 33:11

Praise the unchangeable God! His mercies are everlasting!

GREAT IS YOUR FAITHFULNESS, LORD. AND I AM FOREVER GRATEFUL THAT I CAN KNOW YOU—AND THAT YOUR LOVE AND EXPECTATIONS FOR ME NEVER CHANGE. AMEN.

His Perfect Strength

"My grace is sufficient for you, for my power is made perfect in weakness." Therefore I will boast all the more gladly about my weaknesses, so that Christ's power may rest on me.

2 CORINTHIANS 12:9 NIV

How do you define stress? Perhaps you feel it when the car doesn't start or the toilet backs up or the line is too long at the grocery store. Or maybe your source of stress is a terrible diagnosis, a late-night phone call, a demanding boss, or a broken relationship. It's probably a combination of all of these things. You might be able to cope with one of them, but when several are bearing down at once, stress is the inevitable result.

It has been said that stress results when our perceived demands exceed our perceived resources. When the hours required to meet a deadline at work (demand) exceed the number of hours we have available (resources), we get stressed. The most important word in this definition is *perceived*. When it comes to stress, people have a tendency to do two things. One, they magnify the demand ("I will *never* be able to get this done") and two, they fail to consider all of their resources. For the child of God, this includes His mighty strength, which remains long after ours is gone.

In an uncertain world, it is difficult to say few things for sure. But no matter what life throws our way, we can be confident of this: Our demands will *never* exceed God's vast resources.

STRONG AND MIGHTY HEAVENLY FATHER, THANK YOU THAT IN MY WEAKNESS I CAN ALWAYS RELY ON YOUR PERFECT STRENGTH. AMEN.

Preparing for the Journey Ahead

The Lord *your God has blessed you in all the work of your hands. He has watched over your journey through this vast wilderness. These forty years the* Lord *your God has been with you, and you have not lacked anything.*

Deuteronomy 2:7 niv

If you've ever packed for a vacation, you know what it's like—you stare at mounds of clothes in your suitcase and wonder, *How much of this am I really going to need?*

The truth is, some women over-prepare. We pack too many shoes, too many blouses, too many pieces of jewelry. We're so over-burdened with stuff that the journey gets off to a rocky start.

Now think about this from a spiritual perspective. Picture the Israelites in the wilderness. They could only take with them what they could carry for the journey. Too much baggage and the journey would be slow-going.

If you knew the Lord was about to lead you into a new experience with Him, what would you take with you? Maybe it's time to scale back. Ask God what's important to keep—and what to get rid of. Shake off the nonessentials (things like bitterness, unforgiveness, and anger) and move forward into a new place with the Lord. He will replace those missing items with things like peace, joy, and love. Ah, now that's traveling light!

LORD, I DON'T WANT TO MAKE MY JOURNEY HARDER THAN IT ALREADY IS. I DON'T WANT TO DRAG AROUND WEIGHTY THINGS LIKE BITTERNESS, JEALOUSY, PAIN, AND FRUSTRATION. TODAY I LAY THOSE THINGS DOWN. PLEASE REFILL MY SPIRITUAL LUGGAGE WITH PEACE. JOY. HOPE. GENTLENESS.

The Confession

You, God, know my folly; my guilt is not hidden from you.
PSALM 69:5 NIV

David, the writer of Psalm 69, was in a bad place. He was surrounded by metaphorical water, and yet his thirst could not be quenched. He called out for help, and no one seemed to hear. He was sinking, sinking, and his feet could find no solid ground. His voice had worn out, and his eyes were failing. He claimed that the ones who hated him were too many to count.

And he could have settled there—he could have just blamed all his enemies for his circumstances. He could have pointed the finger at his haters. But instead, he admitted his own guilt. He confessed to God his own foolish choices. And he asked God not to let those who hoped in Him be shamed due to his disgrace.

This is the beauty of knowing and living with God. When your eyes are on Him, you can see your own faults more clearly. But you also have hope that He will not leave you sinking down under the weight of those faults. He will reach down into your sorrow and your remorse and lift you up into His grace.

DEAR LORD WHO SEES ME, HELP MY EYES TO STAY TRAINED ON YOU. AMEN.

As the Son Rises

Now in the morning, having risen a long while before daylight, He went out and departed to a solitary place; and there He prayed.

Mark 1:35 NKJV

After Jesus' baptism, the forty days of temptation, the calling of His disciples, and His walk from Galilee to Capernaum, Jesus heads into the synagogue to teach. Later that afternoon and into the evening, He drives out demons and heals the multitudes. Heaven only knows what time He gets to bed. Yet the next day, Jesus rises before the sun, goes to a deserted place, and prays. There, with Abba God, Jesus receives the strength, power, wisdom, and love He'll need to face the tasks before Him.

How is your daily prayer life? Are you making going to God your first priority? And what happens after you pray? Do you expect anything in your day to change? Are you placing all your hope and expectations in God and His power (Psalm 39:7) or in yourself and your own strength?

Perhaps it's time to change things up, to reenergize your prayer life. Consider setting your alarm five, ten, fifteen, or twenty minutes earlier than usual, giving you time to seek God's face before the husband stirs, the kids clamor for breakfast, or the dog jumps up on your bed.

Today, make it a priority to go to God in prayer, expecting Him to meet all your needs—and more!

FATHER, HELP ME MAKE MEETING ALONE WITH YOU MY FIRST AND MOST BLESSED PRIORITY.

Love Me Steady

For his unfailing love toward those who fear him is as great as the height of the heavens above the earth.

Psalm 103:11 NLT

To err is human, and when we're slumped in the aftermath of our latest sins, there's nothing we'd like more than a clean slate. The trouble is, the devil likes to whisper in our ears. He tells us that heap of shame is where we belong. Worse yet, he tells us God prefers we stay there because a holy God can't look on us with love. Not now.

But that isn't God's truth. Not ever. If you are a trembling heap today, hear God's whispers. Imagine Him speaking His Word to you: "I have not dealt with you according to your sins; nor rewarded you according to your iniquities. For as the heaven is high above the earth, so great is My mercy toward you who fear Me. As far as the east is from the west, so far have I removed your transgressions from you. Like a father pities his children, so I pity you. For I know your frame; I remember that you are dust" (based on Psalm 103:10–14 KJV).

Ask for forgiveness—for the God of mercy and compassion gives it freely. Then stand up—for His love can certainly bear your weight.

GOD, I DON'T UNDERSTAND WHY YOU LOVE ME, BUT I'M SO GRATEFUL THAT YOU DO. FORGIVE MY SINS. HELP ME RISE TALL AND STEADY.

Giver of Good Things

For the LORD *God is a sun and shield; the* LORD *will give grace and glory; no good thing will He withhold from those who walk uprightly.*

PSALM 84:11 NKJV

Worry is such a useless practice, like spinning wheels on a vehicle that takes you nowhere. And yet we women are notorious for it. The Bible advises us to let each day take care of itself. We are promised that God will provide for us.

Psalm 84:11 says that God is not a withholder of good things from His children. He knows us. He created us and put in us our own unique dreams, preferences, and hopes. When you begin to worry, read this verse. Put it on your bulletin board at work and your bathroom mirror at home. Read it aloud each time that worry begins to creep in.

Your heavenly Father is not "the big man upstairs" looking down upon you and laughing at the unfulfilled desires in your life. He wants to give you good things. Often His timing is different than ours, but His plan is always to bless and never to harm us. Look for the blessings in each day and keep bringing your desires before the Lord in expectation.

FATHER, SOMETIMES I WONDER WHY YOU DON'T JUST POUR DOWN FROM HEAVEN THE BLESSING THAT I CRY OUT FOR. GIVE ME PATIENCE, AND HELP ME TO SEE THE GOOD GIFTS, EVEN THE SMALL ONES, FROM YOU IN EACH DAY. AMEN.

God Is in the Details

Give all your worries and cares to God, for he cares about you.
1 PETER 5:7 NLT

Do you ever wonder if God cares about the details of your life?

Take a look at nature. God is definitely a God of details. Notice the various patterns, shapes, and sizes of animals. Their life cycles. The noises they make. Their natural defenses. Details!

Have you wandered through the woods and noticed the towering trees? Their scents? The cool refreshment their shade provides? The different types of leaves, and the tiny, life-bearing veins that run through them? How intricate!

What about the weather? It is filled with details from the hand of your God. The Creator sends raindrops—sometimes gentle and kind, other times harsh and pelting. He warms you with the sun, cools you with breezes, and yes—it is true—He fashions each snowflake, each unique, no two alike! The same way He designs His children!

Do you wonder if God cares about that struggle you are facing at work or the argument you had with a loved one? Is He aware of your desire to find that special someone or the difficulty you have in loving your husband? He cares. Tell him your concerns. He is not too busy to listen to the details. He wants to show Himself real and alive to you in such a way that you know it must be Him. The details of your life are not *little* to God. If they matter to you, they matter to Him.

THANK YOU, LORD, FOR CARING ABOUT THE DETAILS OF MY LIFE. IT MEANS SO MUCH TO KNOW YOU DO. AMEN.

Tried and True

As for God, his way is perfect; the word of the LORD is tried: he is a buckler to all them that trust in him.

2 SAMUEL 22:31 KJV

Amid his many troubles, David, the man after God's own heart, fully believed in God's promises to him. One important promise stands out—that David would be king and there would always be a king from his line on Israel's throne after him—a promise that would culminate in the eternal rule of Jesus, the King of kings (see Psalm 89:28–29; Matthew 1).

If you feel like you are forever waiting and praying for God's promises to be fulfilled in your life, David would understand completely. The psalms show how David wrestled through many bleak days to keep his hope fixed on the Lord. But finally, after being on the run from Saul and fighting numerous enemies, David assumed the throne and sang today's song of praise! David would be quick to tell you that though your hope feels small, his God is trustworthy—He is your strong shield, His promises tried and true.

Today, no matter what you are up against, spend some time with David's song of praise, recounting the victories and grace the Lord has given you. Reminding yourself of His goodness and His help in the past will give you hope for the waiting—just as it did for one famous shepherd-king.

LORD, I PRAISE YOU FOR BEING TRIED AND TRUE!

Morning Guidance

Let me hear of your unfailing love each morning, for I am trusting you. Show me where to walk, for I give myself to you.
Psalm 143:8 NLT

The sunlight stretches through the curtains, into your room, lying warm and golden on the top of your bed. It is a beacon, calling you to sit up and greet the day.

The first light of the day, whether it comes from the lamp beside your bed or from the sunrise, can serve as a reminder that today is a new beginning. The first page of a new chapter. The first line of a new story. Whatever has gone before need not be forgotten—in fact, it's good to remember the days that have passed and to recall the times God has been with you and how He's shown His love each step of the way. And on this new day, in full confidence of His unfailing love, you can commit once again to put your life in His hands. You can trust Him. He will not lead you down a wrong path. He will not leave you to walk any path alone.

When you start the day off in God's Word, you start the day knowing truth, gaining wisdom, and confirming His love for you. Can you think of a better way to begin any adventure?

LORD OF LOVE, CALL ME EVERY MORNING
TO WAKE UP IN YOUR WORD. AMEN.

Listen to Me

I love the Lord because he hears my voice and my prayer for mercy.
Psalm 116:1 NLT

It can be hard to talk to someone you love during an intimate moment or to friends when you're seated at a crowded table or to business associates during a meeting. There may be moments when you feel like you aren't actually being heard. Maybe others are talking over you or simply not understanding how you feel or what you're trying to say. Maybe they simply reject your words altogether. During those moments, you may begin to feel lonely and isolated. You might start thinking your voice doesn't matter.

If anyone has ever told you that you or your voice doesn't matter, know that those words are untrue and come straight from the enemy. You are under no obligation to receive or believe them.

Dear friend, God listens to you. Every day. Every moment. Because you're important to Him. Your Lord wants nothing more than to completely connect with His daughters. Your voice, your ideas, and your feelings are important to Him. Take them to Him at any hour, and He will be there to listen.

DEAR GOD, MY RELATIONSHIPS—EVEN WITH THOSE I LOVE—ARE IMPERFECT ON THIS SIDE OF ETERNITY. BUT YOU, LORD, ARE FOREVER PERFECT. AND WHEREAS SOME PEOPLE MAY IGNORE MY WORDS OR HURT ME WITH THEIR OWN, I KNOW YOU'LL ALWAYS LISTEN TO ME AND NEVER HARM ME. FOR THIS I THANK AND PRAISE YOU. AMEN.

Overwhelmed by Life

"The waves of death swirled about me; the torrents of destruction overwhelmed me. . . . In my distress I called to the LORD. . . . From his temple he heard my voice; my cry came to his ears."

2 SAMUEL 22:5, 7 NIV

Some days the "dailyness" of life seems like a never-ending grind. We get up, eat, work, rest—and do it again the next day. Then when tragedy strikes, we're swept up in grief. What once seemed doable now seems like a huge challenge. Depression sinks its claws deep into our spirits. Fatigue sets in, and we are overwhelmed: Life is hard. We may be tempted to question, "Is this all there is?"

Here's the good news: There's more. God never meant for us to simply exist. He created us for a specific purpose. He longs for us to make a difference and show others His love and grace. What's more, He never asked us to do life alone. When the waves of death swirl around us, and the pounding rain of destruction threatens to overwhelm us, we can cry out to our heavenly Father, knowing that He will not let us drown. He will hear our voice, and He will send help.

So, the next time you feel that you can't put one foot in front of the other, ask God to send you His strength and energy. He will help you to live out your purpose in this chaotic world.

LORD, THANK YOU FOR STRENGTHENING ME WHEN THE "DAILYNESS" OF LIFE, AND ITS VARIOUS TRIALS, THREATENS TO OVERWHELM ME.

Finding Peace

And he will be called. . .Prince of Peace.
ISAIAH 9:6 NIV

We all long for a peaceful place. The desire for peace is etched into our genetic code. . .perhaps because we're made in God's image and He is full of peace. When we think of peace, our minds fill with images of calm, quiet serenity. We picture a hilltop, surrounded by lovely gardens, with birds singing and loved ones laughing gently.

While it's good to seek out a peaceful, tranquil existence, that's not always possible. In this world, stress finds us. War happens. People can be mean and selfish. Diseases appear, accidents occur. So how can we have peace when the pressures and tensions of life seem to hunt us down?

It's possible to have peace in the midst of chaos when we understand where peace is found. God's peace isn't confined to a specific location or a specific set of circumstances. His peace isn't something we have to maneuver and create. Jesus Christ is the Prince of Peace. Peace is His kingdom, and as long as He lives within us, that is where His peace dwells.

It's important to walk away from stress when we can. But when stress finds us, we can extinguish it—or at least diminish it greatly—by calling on the Prince of Peace within our hearts. When we respond with the calm, quiet assurance that comes from Christ alone, we will find peace.

DEAR FATHER, THANK YOU FOR SENDING THE PRINCE OF PEACE. HELP ME TO CALL ON HIM WHEN I NEED PEACE. AMEN.

Right on Time

He asked her, "Woman, why are you crying? Who is it you are looking for?" Thinking he was the gardener, she said, "Sir, if you have carried him away, tell me where you have put him, and I will get him." Jesus said to her, "Mary." She turned toward him and cried out in Aramaic, "Rabboni!" (which means "Teacher").

John 20:15–16 niv

Surely you have wondered why Mary assumed Jesus was the gardener. Was it because He spoke from behind her (see John 20:14), or was it because she didn't expect Him that she didn't recognize Him? But the fact remains: There she was, mourning Jesus, and suddenly *there He was*. Instead of chiding her for not believing His words, Mary's loving Savior comforted her, dispelling the grief from her heart and replacing it with joy—and purpose. Jesus told her to bear witness to His resurrection by telling the disciples she had seen Him.

On your heavy-heart days, you might not really expect Jesus to show up. But turn around, dear friend! Your Savior calls you by name, and His grace is always right on time. Think back on how Jesus has renewed your joy in the past: sending just the right scripture, a call from a friend, or a surprise refund when your paycheck was beyond stretched. Like Mary, bear witness to His love and presence today!

THANK YOU, JESUS, THAT YOU ARE ALWAYS ON TIME. YOUR GRACE IS ENOUGH; YOU ARE ENOUGH.

Forget Not His Benefits

Bless the Lord, *O my soul, and forget not all His benefits: who forgives all your iniquities, who heals all your diseases, who redeems your life from destruction, who crowns you with lovingkindness and tender mercies, who satisfies your mouth with good things, so that your youth is renewed like the eagle's.*

Psalm 103:2–5 NKJV

Your friendship with the Creator of the universe comes with many benefits that are simply out of this world. Did you know, for example, that God not only forgives all of your sins, but He's a healer of diseases, a Redeemer from destruction, a crowner of loving-kindness, and the ultimate satisfaction? He's the be-all and end-all, capable of fulfilling every need you could ever have in your life—emotional, physical, or spiritual.

Why does God offer so much to those He loves? Because He's a good, good Father. And it doesn't stop there. He longs for complete renewal in your life. He's waiting for you to take off like an eagle, soaring over your circumstances. It all starts with your acceptance of His benefits. So what are you waiting for? Spread those wings and fly, girl!

FATHER, I DON'T DESERVE YOUR GOODNESS, BUT YOU LAVISH IT ON ME ANYWAY. THANK YOU FROM THE BOTTOM OF MY HEART—NOT JUST FOR YOUR BENEFITS BUT FOR YOUR NEVER-ENDING LOVE. I'M SO BLESSED, LORD. AMEN.

The Love of God

May the Lord lead your hearts into a full understanding and expression of the love of God.
2 THESSALONIANS 3:5 NLT

God loves you.

Maybe you've known this since you were a tiny child, but despite its simplicity, God's love is so vast—so wonderfully mysterious—that it'll take a lifetime (plus eternity) to understand it fully.

Today, meditate on these truths:

- The LORD is compassionate and merciful, slow to get angry and filled with unfailing love (Psalm 103:8 NLT).
- He heals the brokenhearted and bandages their wounds (Psalm 147:3 NLT).
- Nothing in all creation will ever be able to separate us from the love of God (Romans 8:39 NLT).
- For this is how God loved the world: He gave his one and only Son, so that everyone who believes in him will not perish but have eternal life (John 3:16 NLT).
- But God is so rich in mercy, and he loved us so much, that even though we were dead because of our sins, he gave us life when he raised Christ from the dead (Ephesians 2:4–5 NLT).

There is no better place for you to be and no more secure situation than resting in the love of God.

GOD, TEACH ME TO UNDERSTAND YOUR LOVE MORE FULLY.

Look Around

Come and see the works of God; He is awesome in His doing toward the sons of men.
Psalm 66:5 NKJV

We tend to think of encouragement as coming in the way of cards, phone calls, gifts, or efforts performed on our behalf. Isn't it wonderful how God uses people to encourage us? But when the cards or calls don't come, we're wise to look at the other ways God can send us encouragement.

First, He uplifts us through His Word. Just by reading the Bible, we're reminded of the grace and love God has for us. Then there's His creation. Watching a bird fly, seeing a squirrel scramble up a tree, and observing a beautiful flower or a wonderful sunrise are just a few ways God reminds us of His power. Encouragement can also be found by remembering what God has done for us.

If it's been a while since you received a phone call, visit, or card, don't grow discouraged, thinking that God isn't aware of your needs. He's creative in His encouragement—just take the time to look for it.

DEAR GOD, I THANK YOU FOR ALL THE WAYS YOU ENCOURAGE ME. MAY I NOT OVERLOOK YOUR BLESSINGS BECAUSE THEY DIDN'T COME IN THE FORM I EXPECTED.

Pressing On

I press on to take hold of that for which
Christ Jesus took hold of me.
PHILIPPIANS 3:12 NIV

We all need a lot of work when it comes to fulfilling God's perfect plan for our lives. We get sidetracked, we mess up, life distracts us . . .and progress is slow. No matter how sincere our desire to live out God's purpose for us, we fall down again. And again.

But that's okay. God knows us better than anyone, and He knows we're not perfect. He knows we'll make mistakes and have setbacks. All He asks is that each time we fall down, we get back up and keep moving forward.

Think about it. Christ saw potential in us—so much that He died for us. He didn't say, "Oh good grief, look how slow they are! Look at how many times they goof up. Never mind. It's not worth it." Nope. He paid such a high price for us because He knew we were made in His image. And He knew that as long as we trust Him, don't give up, and keep pressing forward, our likeness will become closer and closer to His.

That's what He wants for us—for our spirits to mirror His. He wants us to love, for He is love. He wants us to be kind and gentle and compassionate, for He is all those things. He longs for us to be His representatives in this world. And we will be, as long as we keep pressing on.

DEAR FATHER, HELP ME TO PRESS ON TO BECOME MORE LIKE YOU. AMEN.

Plan to Trust

The LORD knows all human plans; he knows that they are futile.
PSALM 94:11 NIV

Ever have your plans blow up in your face? In 1 Kings 12, King Jeroboam of Israel had a pretty good plan to keep his kingship out of trouble, but it backfired in a big way. God had promised a throne for Jeroboam and his descendants if he was obedient to His commands, but Jeroboam was worried about one little detail—the temple in Jerusalem. He feared that if his people traveled to Judah to worship, they would defect to King Rehoboam, his rival. So Jeroboam made golden calves in Israel as a stand-in for the temple. Like Aaron in the time of the Exodus, Jeroboam severely disobeyed God's commands by doing this, and while it didn't happen immediately, his kingly line disintegrated.

Certainly, you have made plans for a secure life: working toward a full savings account or keeping your family healthy or other good goals. But what's driving your plans—fear of the future or faith that God's grace will be there for you in the future? Every Christian struggles with this. But relying on anything for security apart from God never ends well. . .and it puts distance between you and Him. Where is fear steering your way? Pour out your worries to God, and He will restore your heart with His abiding peace (see John 16:33).

JESUS, HELP ME TRUST YOU; TEACH MY HEART TO EXPECT YOUR GRACE IN WHAT'S AHEAD.

That New Covenant Smell

The old system under the law of Moses was only a shadow, a dim preview of the good things to come, not the good things themselves. The sacrifices under that system were repeated again and again, year after year, but they were never able to provide perfect cleansing for those who came to worship.

HEBREWS 10:1 NLT

Sometimes it's good to do with what we already have. Maybe it's not the newest, shiniest, or fanciest thing around, but it works well enough (mostly), and we can get by.

But when we're talking about the old covenant (priests and sacrifices and atonement and ceremonial washing and more) in contrast to the new covenant, there's no comparing the two. The writer of Hebrews describes the old way as "only a shadow, a dim preview of the good things to come." The heroes of the faith (mentioned in Hebrews 11) from the old covenant accepted and lived within the law and got a small taste of God's glory. But we who live under the new covenant can receive the perfect cleansing that Jesus' sacrifice on the cross gives us.

God offers you the best, the most perfect new life that you could never hope to earn on your own. Don't make do with what you already have when it comes to your faith. Accept God's grace, His cleansing, and His new mercies every day (Lamentations 3:23).

NEW COVENANT GOD, THANK YOU FOR MAKING A NEW WAY—THE BEST WAY—JESUS. AMEN.

Three Things

O people, the LORD *has told you what is good,*
and this is what he requires of you: to do what is right,
to love mercy, and to walk humbly with your God.
MICAH 6:8 NLT

What three things does God require of you?

1. to do what is right
2. to love mercy
3. to walk humbly with Him

Now, for an even more important question: *How* can you accomplish these three things in your life? There are some prerequisites. Most important is a right relationship with God as your Father—because from this, all else will flow. Without this relationship, it's impossible to meet all of His requirements.

So today, focus on this one thing: your connection to the heavenly Father. Ask Him for His help, and then commit to doing the work it takes to make your relationship stronger than it is right this very moment. Once you've established a firm and unshakable faith foundation, you'll see just how naturally the three requirements of God come to you. And truly, there's no better example to follow than Jesus for a life well lived!

FATHER GOD, I WANT TO PLEASE YOU TODAY AND ALL MY DAYS. IT'S MY DESIRE TO MEET YOUR REQUIREMENTS—AND TO DO ALL THINGS WELL. HELP ME TO STAY STRONG IN MY COMMITMENT TO YOU, LORD. WITH YOU BY MY SIDE, I CAN ACCOMPLISH ALL YOU EXPECT AND ASK OF ME. AMEN.

Jesus' Wristwatch

Look carefully then how you walk, not as unwise but as wise, making the best use of the time, because the days are evil. Therefore do not be foolish, but understand what the will of the Lord is.

EPHESIANS 5:15–17 ESV

Time is money, they say. Society preaches the value of making good use of our time—and the expense of wasting it.

In the Bible, Ephesians 5 speaks of using every opportunity wisely. But even though scripture teaches the value of time, Jesus never wore a watch. He didn't view His opportunities within the bounds of earthly time.

Have you ever ended a day with guilt and regret over the growing black hole of work yet to be completed? Or do you feel peace at the end of your day, having walked in the presence of the Lord?

Satan wants to consume you with endless lists of meaningless tasks. Fight back! Concern yourself less with the items you can cross off your to-do list, and more with those things the Lord would have you spend your time and energy on. You can strive to be a great multitasker or workhorse—but it's more important and fulfilling to be an efficient laborer for the Lord.

FATHER, HELP ME TO SEE WHERE YOU ARE WORKING AND JOIN YOU THERE. LET ME PLACE MY LIST OF TASKS ASIDE AS I SEEK YOUR WILL FOR ME TODAY. THEN GIVE ME THE ABILITY TO SHOW MYSELF GRACE FOR THE THINGS I DO NOT GET DONE.

Laughing at the Days to Come

She is clothed with strength and dignity;
she can laugh at the days to come.
PROVERBS 31:25 NIV

You mean a woman of God can laugh at the days to come? Really? Wow. Most of the world wakes up each morning under a black cloud of regret and a debilitating fear of the future. That sounds more realistic, right? To laugh at the future is hard to imagine. To see hope instead of futility? Promise in the pain? What would that kind of woman look like? Sound like?

Perhaps a woman of God as described in Proverbs 31 doesn't necessarily have a lot of confidence in herself, but rather in God. Perhaps she trusts so implicitly in His divine plan and goodness that she can sleep deeply. She can wake up refreshed each morning.

And this woman of God knows some truths—that God will indeed work everything for good in her life. That He is watching over her comings and goings, and nothing will befall her that He can't handle. She knows that this earthly life is temporary. That heaven is not only for real but forever. Knowing these truths all the way to her soul gives her peace and joy, and it shows in her countenance. Yes, and even in her laugh.

JESUS, HELP ME TRUST IN YOU EVERY HOUR OF EVERY DAY, AND LET ME BE SO FULL OF PEACE THAT I TOO CAN LAUGH AT THE DAYS TO COME. AMEN.

Celebrate Justice. . .and Grace

So the king died and was brought to Samaria, and they buried him there. They washed the chariot at a pool in Samaria. . .and the dogs licked up his blood, as the word of the LORD had declared.

1 KINGS 22:37–38 NIV

The prophecy made Ahab quake in his sandals—his kingly line would fall, and the dogs would lap up his blood (see 1 Kings 21:19–22). Well aware of the trouble he was in, Ahab tried to escape his fate by dressing up like a common soldier when he went to battle, but an arrow drawn "at random" caught him "between the sections of his armor" (22:34 NIV), showing that God's justice cannot be fooled.

Maybe you did a little victory dance when you read that Ahab got what he deserved. But. . .have you considered your sins' consequences recently? Surely you haven't stolen and committed murder as Ahab did, but sin in any form creates distance between you and God and hurts those around you. And its consequences reverberate. So celebrate His justice, but be sure to fall on His grace.

As you come into God's presence through Jesus, confess your sins with reverence and awe for His unfathomable holiness and grace, and be restored. Humbly thank Him for the forgiveness He gave in Christ—because you have only escaped the true weight of justice through grace.

FATHER, LET ME NEVER FORGET THAT MY RELATIONSHIP WITH YOU WAS BOUGHT BY JESUS' SACRIFICE.

Unfailing Love

LORD, do not rebuke me in your anger or discipline me in your wrath. Have mercy on me, LORD, for I am faint; heal me, LORD, for my bones are in agony. My soul is in deep anguish. How long, LORD, how long? Turn, LORD, and deliver me; save me because of your unfailing love.

PSALM 6:1–4 NIV

David was deeply anguished. Thoughts of his sinful state likely kept him up at night. His troubles weighed heavily on his soul. His words here in Psalm 6 reveal his absolute dread of God's anger and discipline. In fact, David was begging for God's mercy.

And after airing his negative thoughts and feelings, David then acknowledged that God was fully capable of delivering him from his torment. Because God is a God of "unfailing love," David knew, without a doubt, that all would be well if it was God's will for his life. And that was that!

Like David, do thoughts of your sinful past interfere with a good night's sleep? Do your troubles weigh heavily on your spirit? Today is the day to approach the heavenly Father in bold confidence. Let Him know that you trust Him with the outcome. . .you trust Him to see you through to better days ahead. He will hear you, and He will act. Praise Him!

HEAVENLY FATHER, I TRUST YOU FOR MY COMFORT. . .FOR DELIVERANCE FROM MY TROUBLES. THANK YOU FOR SAVING ME!

Words to Live By

When the soldiers crucified Jesus, they took his clothes, dividing them into four shares, one for each of them, with the undergarment remaining. This garment was seamless, woven in one piece from top to bottom. "Let's not tear it," they said to one another. "Let's decide by lot who will get it." This happened that the scripture might be fulfilled.

John 19:23–24 NIV

How did Jesus' followers react as they watched His crucifixion? Some were probably brokenhearted at the sight of the Savior's suffering. Still others probably panicked, thinking all their hopes were dying on that cross. But the ones who were paying attention would have seen that everything was going as expected.

God foreknew every detail of that dreadful day—down to the soldiers divvying up Jesus' clothes. Centuries earlier, David had written, "They pierce my hands and my feet. . . . They divide my clothes among them and cast lots for my garment" (Psalm 22:16, 18 NIV).

In trying times, we may be so focused on the trouble that we miss God's messages. No, the details of our particular troubles aren't predicted in the Bible, but God has given us details about who He is in *any* trouble—He is omniscient, trustworthy, all-powerful, compassionate—and those details see us through the trouble. Rest in His Word. All is going according to His plan.

GOD, MAKE YOUR MESSAGES CLEAR TO ME AS I READ THE BIBLE. ENCOURAGE ME WITH YOUR WORDS.

Why Me?

I am Alpha and Omega, the beginning and the ending.
REVELATION 1:8 KJV

Many people look at difficult circumstances selfishly and cry: "Oh, God, why me? Why do these things happen to *me*?"

But we mortals have a too-narrow view of our existence. In our minds, it can seem at points that this world is all there is. Sure, God is eternal—but maybe that just means He was around before us and envisioned that we would come into being someday.

If that's our concept of God, we need to read His Word more closely.

Jesus said He is the "Alpha and Omega." He's the beginning and the end. Jesus, like the Father, *is*. He is the ever-present one who is apart from time.

When God spoke our world into existence, He called into being a certain reality, knowing then everything that ever was to happen—and everyone who ever was to be.

That you exist now is cause for rejoicing! God made *you* to fellowship with Him! If that fellowship demands trials for a season, rejoice that God thinks you worthy to share in the sufferings of Christ—and, eventually, in His glory.

Why do these things happen to you?

Because God in His infinite wisdom, love, and grace determined them to be. Praise His holy name!

FATHER, SHINE THROUGH ALL MY TRIALS TODAY. I WANT YOU TO GET THE GLORY.

Women Transformed by Grace

Soon afterward, Jesus began going around from one city and village to another, proclaiming and preaching the kingdom of God. The twelve were with Him, and also some women who had been healed of evil spirits and sicknesses: Mary who was called Magdalene, from whom seven demons had gone out, and Joanna the wife of Chuza, Herod's steward, and Susanna, and many others who were contributing to their support out of their private means.

LUKE 8:1–3 NASB

The scriptural account records that Jesus changed the lives of all who came into contact with Him. Some of these He changed simply by entering their world, and others were changed in more dramatic ways. Of course, Mary, His mother, was the first woman whose life was radically altered by His incarnation. The sisters Mary and Martha knew Him as a frequent guest and friend. Other women contributed to His ministry and daily life through financial support; and they followed Him, weeping, as He carried His cross and came with spices to prepare His body that misty third morning.

There were still other women besides Mary whose lives He drastically changed—the woman at the well in Samaria, the woman caught in adultery and thrown at His feet, the widow whose son He raised from the dead, and the woman with the bleeding disorder who was made well from touching His robe. As Creator, Jesus understood the inner longings of a woman's heart and offered redemption for hurts and the promise of hope and healing. And He still does today.

JESUS, THANK YOU FOR UNDERSTANDING ME AND FOR GIVING YOUR LIFE TO REDEEM ME. PLEASE TRANSFORM ME WITH YOUR GRACE. AMEN.

All Fall, All Free

All have sinned and fall short of the glory of God, and all are justified freely by his grace through the redemption that came by Christ Jesus.

ROMANS 3:23–24 NIV

Several verses in Romans are often used as a kind of shorthand for sharing the gospel of Jesus Christ. The verses above are the starting point—they describe the state of human beings. *All* have sinned. *All* fall short. There are no divisions between those who have sinned a lot and those who have sinned a little. Murderers, liars, adulterers, and gossipers are all thrown into the same group. If you have ever known a right thing to do and chosen instead to do wrong, you have sinned (see James 4:17). If you are human, you have sinned. And if you have sinned, you are not worthy of the glory of God.

But thankfully the story doesn't stop there. Everyone has fallen, but you can be made worthy by the gift of the grace of God. It's a mysterious gift—one that doesn't just add to who you are or what you have, like other possessions that bestow some added honor or wealth. It's a gift that changes where you stand. Without this grace, you sink to the bottom of the sea. With it, you can walk on water to meet your Savior.

GOD, THANK YOU FOR OFFERING ME THE GIFT OF GRACE! AMEN.

Long Fuse

You, O God, are both tender and kind, not easily angered, immense in love, and you never, never quit.

PSALM 86:15 MSG

We all know someone who has a short fuse. The one who, at the smallest traffic delay or offense, loses her temper. Or turns red if she has to wait at the store checkout or gets a glare from a fellow shopper. She's the one others have to watch their words around for fear of setting her off.

Thankfully, the Bible says God has a long fuse—that He's slow to get angry (Exodus 34:6; Numbers 14:18; Nehemiah 9:17; Psalm 103:8; Joel 2:13; Jonah 4:2; Nahum 1:3). Yet does the fact that God has lots of patience mean we should give ourselves a pass when it comes to sin? Certainly not!

God's desire is for our salvation through Jesus Christ and adopting as many children into His family who'll accept His gift of grace. He knows we aren't perfect—but His love is.

Ask God to show you where you might need to repent, remembering He's not angry. He's just waiting in compassion and mercy to give you the full life He's designed for you.

GOD, YOU'VE EVERY RIGHT TO GET FRUSTRATED WITH ME WHEN I MESS UP, BUT YOUR PATIENT MERCY AND LOVE ARE GREATER THAN YOUR ANGER. CLEAN MY HANDS AND FACE AND PURIFY MY HEART, FATHER. I DON'T WANT ANY SIN TO STAND BETWEEN US. AMEN.

God and Father

The Lord *reigns, let the nations tremble; he sits enthroned between the cherubim, let the earth shake.*

Psalm 99:1 niv

God is our heavenly Father. He is a God who dries tears, who sends His Spirit to comfort us, who enfolds us in the shelter of His wings. He calls us to His side as a dad calls his children, and we can call back, "Abba—Daddy!" Yet He is more. He is God Almighty. "Great is the Lord," the psalmist wrote; "the Lord our God is holy" (Psalm 99:2, 9 niv). God is lofty, and down here entire nations tremble and the earth shakes as a result.

When the Bible speaks of fearing God, it doesn't mean better-run-and-hide fear; it means the awe and respect that overcome us in God's presence. And that kind of fear actually ends the run-and-hide kind, no matter where it surfaces in our lives. How can that be? Because God is both mighty God *and* loving Father. He has the ability and desire to hear us whenever we pray—as well as the power and compassion to answer. He is holy and He is forgiving. He is the steady pillar that points out the way, all the while reminding us that we are not alone along the way. There's just no other God like Him!

GOD, I AM AMAZED BY ALL YOU ARE. AND I AM SO GLAD THAT YOU ARE MY GOD AND FATHER.

I Am a Friend of God

When Jesus saw their faith, he said,
"Friend, your sins are forgiven."
LUKE 5:20 NIV

Friendships are critical to women, and godly friendships are the best. Can you even imagine a world without your girlfriends in it? Impossible! Who would you share your hopes and dreams with? Your goals and aspirations? Oh, what a blessing women of God are! They breathe hope and life into us when we need it most. They laugh along with us at chick flicks. They cry with us when our hearts are broken.

Isn't it amazing to realize God calls us His friends? He reaches out to us with a friendship that goes above and beyond the very best the world has to offer. Best of all, He's not the sort of friend who loses touch or forgets to call. He's always there. And while your earthly friends might do a good job of comforting you when you're down, their brand of comfort doesn't even begin to compare with the Lord's. He knows just what to say when things go wrong, and He knows how to throw an amazing celebration when things go well for you.

Today, thank the Lord—not just for salvation, not just for the work He's done in your heart, not just for the people and things He's placed in your life—but for calling you His friend.

O, LORD, I'M SO BLESSED TO BE CALLED YOUR FRIEND! YOU'RE THE BEST ONE I'LL EVER HAVE. THANK YOU FOR THE KIND OF FRIENDSHIP THAT SUPERSEDES ALL BOUNDARIES.

A Fresh Start

"See, I am doing a new thing! Now it springs up; do you not perceive it? I am making a way in the wilderness and streams in the wasteland."

ISAIAH 43:19 NIV

There is something about a fresh beginning. At the start of the new year, people decide to make positive changes in their lives. The new year seems to usher in another round of hope for achievement and organization—for a while at least.

God specializes in giving us a new start. Lamentations 3:22–23 tells us that His compassion is new every morning. We can never make a mistake so big that God can't give us a fresh start. Nothing is too big for the blood of Jesus to cover. He wants to give us new lives right where we are.

As we trust in Him, He will make us into new creatures. That's not something we can do ourselves. Our pasts can't hold us back. While Satan loves to remind us of our pasts and the mistakes we've made, God is turning the wildernesses of our lives into beautiful growth with His living water. Remember to trust God for the changes He is making in you and to thank Him for His unfailing love.

HEAVENLY FATHER, WE THANK YOU THAT YOUR LOVE NEVER RUNS OUT ON US. THANK YOU FOR COVERING OUR SINS WITH THE BLOOD OF YOUR SON AND GIVING US NEW LIFE EVERY DAY. AMEN.

Access Door

Therefore, since we have been justified through faith, we have peace with God through our Lord Jesus Christ, through whom we have gained access by faith into this grace in which we now stand.

ROMANS 5:1–2 NIV

Through a labyrinth of dark hallways and secret doors you come. It seems you may never find a way out. But finally the shadowy space in front of you opens a little, and one last door appears. A few steps lead up to a wider area still. You move your hands along the velvety curtains until you find the seam that marks the center of the stage. Then, as you inhale deeply, the bright lights switch on, the curtains pull away, and there you are—standing in the spotlight.

Accepting Jesus as your Lord and Savior gives you special access to the center stage of God's theater. You don't have to stay in the shadows watching a more joy-filled life go by. God invites you to step into His light and live boldly in the scenes He has written just for you. He is your director and guide, your manager and your adoring audience. And He is the author of your life, the gifter of grace.

Though you may sometimes get butterflies in your stomach, you don't have to be afraid to use your voice. You can find peace in the certainty that God will be with you, every minute.

GOD, THANK YOU FOR THE GRACE IN WHICH I STAND. AMEN.

Spring in Your Step

Praise ye the Lord. *O give thanks unto the* Lord; *for he is good: for his mercy endureth for ever. Who can utter the mighty acts of the* Lord? *who can shew forth all his praise?*

Psalm 106:1–2 KJV

What prompts you to praise God when all is going well? What prompts your praise when things aren't going well? Is it listening to other people's testimonies? Recalling the times God has been faithful to you? Hearing an encouraging message preached? What gives you the glimpse of hope and encouragement you're craving?

In the early days of the church, a message was delivered to the Antioch believers, bringing the new Christians great joy as it was read aloud. Then the prophets Judas and Silas spoke to "the believers, encouraging and strengthening their faith" (Acts 15:32 NLT).

If you need an extra dose of support and encouragement, consider tapping into old messages that have buoyed your faith in the past—or seek out new ones. As you do so, God's joy will bubble up within you, giving you that extra spring in your step and prompting praise to roll off your lips.

FATHER GOD, WHETHER I'M IN A SEASON OF HARVEST OR A SEASON OF DROUGHT, HELP ME TO PRAISE YOU. IF JOYFUL WORDS ARE NOT FLOWING FROM MY MOUTH, HELP ME GET THERE BY READING OR HEARING THE ENCOURAGING MESSAGES OF OTHERS OR BY DRAWING FROM THE ENCOURAGEMENT OF GOD'S WORD.

Don't Forget

Praise the L*ORD*, *my soul; all my inmost being, praise his holy name. Praise the* L*ORD*, *my soul, and forget not all his benefits.*

PSALM 103:1–2 NIV

The phrase "praise the Lord" is found scores of times in the psalms, whether things were good—or bad. How is praise possible when our world is in turmoil? How is praise possible when all that meets our eyes is negative? We must choose to keep God's blessings in mind, to think on all God does. That's what David did. He told his soul to praise and to forget not. . .

Forget not that God forgives every sin—even the ones we have a hard time letting go of ourselves. Forget not that God heals us, body and soul. Forget not that God redeems our lives from the deep, dank, dark pit. Forget not that God then crowns us with love, with compassion that we don't deserve but that we need desperately. Forget not that God satisfies our desires with good things—yes, the *best* things—so that we are renewed like eagles soaring high above it all (see Psalm 103:3–5).

In light of God's benefits, nothing on earth can douse our praise if we don't allow it. And nothing on earth can take God's benefits away.

GOD, WHATEVER HAPPENS AROUND ME OR TO ME, YOUR BENEFITS ARE FOR SURE. PRAISE THE LORD, MY SOUL—AND THERE IS SO MUCH TO PRAISE HIM FOR!

Guilt-Free

So now there is no condemnation for those who belong to Christ Jesus.

ROMANS 8:1 NLT

Every one of us has messed up—some of us big-time. Fortunately, we serve the God of second chances.

John tells us in 1 John 1:9, "If we confess our sins, he is faithful and just and will forgive us our sins and purify us from all unrighteousness" (NIV).

When we confess our failures, repent, and move on, God wipes those mistakes away—He sees the children He created, who are washed in the blood of Jesus.

"Therefore," Romans 8:1 says, "[there is] now no condemnation (no adjudging guilty of wrong) for those who are in Christ Jesus, who live [and] walk not after the dictates of the flesh, but after the dictates of the Spirit" (AMPC).

Whatever we've done wrong, let's stop condemning ourselves. If we've confessed those sins, there is no need for our feelings of guilt.

Guilt has held back the blessings of God long enough! Let it go! Have faith in the blood that cleanses *all* sins—past, present, and future.

"Even if we feel guilty, God is greater than our feelings, and he knows everything" (1 John 3:20 NLT).

FATHER GOD, I THANK YOU THAT YOU HAVE FORGIVEN ME. HELP ME TO FORGIVE MYSELF—AND TO LET GO OF THE GUILT THAT KEEPS ME FROM BECOMING THE PERSON YOU SAY THAT I AM. YOUR WORD IS TRUE, AND I CHOOSE TO BELIEVE WHAT YOU SAY OVER WHAT I FEEL.

Rejoice!

Always be full of joy in the Lord. I say it again—rejoice!
PHILIPPIANS 4:4 NLT

Do you feel like life is a fifty-pound backpack? Life can get "heavy" if we aren't careful, with everyday worries wearing us down and making us exhausted. Even small decisions tend to grow in our minds to be more important than they really are. Big decisions can completely take us over so that even the most wonderful news becomes tainted.

Look away from the cares of this world! Rejoice in what the Lord has done! Instead of lending every thought to the troubles at hand, praise God for the ways He has provided in the past and doubtless will provide again in the future!

Begin to count your blessings and feel the weight lifting off your shoulders. Feel the freedom you have to enjoy your life. Enjoy your home and the comfort it brings. Enjoy your family, pets, and the things you have. Allow yourself to fully feel the joy that comes with the first snow, the first warm breeze of spring, or the first rays of sun in the morning. There are so many wonderful things to enjoy even as you read this!

Life is complicated, yes. But it should never be allowed to rob you of the joy the Lord provides. "I say it again—rejoice!"

LORD, YOU ARE SO GOOD! TEACH ME YOUR WAYS AND SHOW ME YOUR FAITHFULNESS, THAT I MAY BE FULL OF JOY BECAUSE OF YOU. YOU CREATED THIS EARTH TO BE ENJOYED, AND ENJOY IT I SHALL!

God's Grace Through the Detour

But he said to me, "My grace is sufficient for you, for my power is made perfect in weakness." Therefore I will boast all the more gladly about my weaknesses, so that Christ's power may rest on me.

2 CORINTHIANS 12:9 NIV

You may be struggling. A situation is out of your control. Someone has made a decision that affects you—and you are not very happy about it.

Take heart. Such things happen often throughout life. You thought you were on a particular path, but the plans, circumstances, or parameters changed. And right now you may feel as though God interrupted your life. But here's the thing: God always has permission to interrupt. And even though you may be having a hard time understanding what it all means, rest assured that you are just on a detour right now—and you cannot detour out of the reach of God's grace.

So there's no need to worry—a detour always puts you right back on the path you are supposed to be on!

Your job is just to take this time to relax, trust Him, and enjoy the scenery.

GOD ALMIGHTY, WHEN YOU INTERRUPT MY LIFE WITH A DETOUR, HELP ME TO EMBRACE IT. I CHOOSE TO TRUST YOU TO TAKE CARE OF THE DETAILS. I LET GO OF THE EXPECTATIONS I HAVE FOR THIS JOURNEY. HELP ME TO LIVE IN THE MOMENT AND EXPERIENCE YOUR GRACE ALONG THE WAY.

God-Confidence

When God our Savior revealed his kindness and love, he saved us, not because of the righteous things we had done, but because of his mercy. He washed away our sins, giving us a new birth and new life through the Holy Spirit. . . . Because of his grace he made us right in his sight and gave us confidence that we will inherit eternal life.

TITUS 3:4–5, 7 NLT

When do you feel most confident? Whether it's some aspect of your career or ministry or hobby, your confidence shines brightest when you're doing something you're exceptionally good at. Confidence is empowering. Confidence is a great feeling.

But none of us are perfect, and we all have bad days that cause us to question if we know what we're doing. Setbacks can leave us frustrated and wondering why we even try.

That's why God's grace is so important in every aspect of our lives. Our old lives had moments of greatness, but ultimately, they were empty and worthless. Our new lives when we're born again are perfect and whole because Jesus Christ is perfect and whole. So we never have to wonder if we're good enough or if our self-confidence can carry us through. Our God-confidence empowers us in this moment and through all of eternity.

FATHER, FILL ME WITH THE GOD-CONFIDENCE THAT I NEED TODAY. LET YOUR MERCY AND GRACE FILL MY HEART AND MY SOUL. BREATHE IN ME A NEW LIFE EVERY MOMENT OF EVERY DAY. AMEN.

Security Blanket

Grace (favor and spiritual blessing) to you and [heart] peace from God our Father and the Lord Jesus Christ (the Messiah, the Anointed One). Blessed be the God and Father of our Lord Jesus Christ, the Father of sympathy (pity and mercy) and the God [Who is the Source] of every comfort (consolation and encouragement).

2 CORINTHIANS 1:2–3 AMPC

There's something to be said for the feelings of serenity and security while snuggled in a plush comforter on a wintry day. You wrap yourself up in its warmth and feel at peace. Being enveloped in the loving arms of God is like that. He brings a feeling of serenity and peace to your heart that overcomes any trouble in your soul.

Each day, say a prayer of thanks for your blessings, beginning with the gift of Jesus Christ. For it's His presence that warms you from the inside out. He's a gift that no one can ever take away. With Jesus in your heart, you can face and do anything.

Praise God for the gift of His Son every day. Doing so will remind you that because Jesus is in your life, you're never alone. And His compassion, His love—they are all yours. Your gratitude and faith are all that's asked in exchange.

GOD, YOUR LOVE AND WARMTH ARE MY COMFORT AND STRENGTH. THANK YOU FOR THE GIFT OF YOUR SON, RESIDING WITHIN MY HEART, BLESSING ME WITH PEACE AND ENCOURAGEMENT. AMEN.

Present Help

For I, the LORD *your God, hold your right hand; it is I who say to you, "Fear not, I am the one who helps you."*

ISAIAH 41:13 ESV

We shake hands to greet each other; it's a sign of welcome. We reach for the hand of a child when we're walking in a crowd or near a street; it helps protect and comfort the child. In times of great emotion or anticipation, we grab the hand of a nearby friend or family member; it says, "I am with you." By a hospital bed, we clasp the hand of a sick loved one; it tells them we are present, suffering with them. With every gripping of another's hand, we are bearing witness to God.

He holds your hand. He welcomes you into His kingdom. He protects you. He comforts you. He is with you in your most anxious moments and in your darkest hours. With the clasp of His hand comes courage for any situation. He tells you not to fear, for He is your ever-present help in times of trouble. He has a hold of you.

ALMIGHTY GOD, I AM GRATEFUL THAT YOU HOLD MY HAND. FORGIVE ME FOR THE TIMES I HAVE FORGOTTEN THIS AND LET FEAR REIGN IN MY LIFE. HELP ME TO REMEMBER I AM NEVER ALONE. GRANT ME THE COURAGE THAT COMES FROM KNOWING YOU AS MY HELPER.

New Every Morning

This I recall to my mind, therefore I have hope.
Through the Lord's mercies we are not consumed,
because His compassions fail not. They are new
every morning; great is Your faithfulness.
Lamentations 3:21–23 NKJV

For many people, one of the most difficult times of the day is nighttime. We fall into bed physically exhausted, grateful to finally be done with the activity of the day. Suddenly our brains are awake and alert with swirling thoughts. Thoughts of today lead to thoughts of yesterday and ten years back. We think of things we should have said but didn't, and things we shouldn't have said but did. We rehearse bad decisions and mistakes and worry anxiously about the future. The thoughts that keep us awake some nights can be daunting, to say the least. These thoughts can consume us with worry, fear, and regret, robbing us of peace and sleep. We feel hopeless and exhausted.

But God's Word says we don't have to be consumed by regrets from the past or fears about the future. Every morning with the rising of the sun comes a new measure of His mercy, compassion, and faithfulness. So let your worrisome thoughts go and replace them with hope. His mercy and compassion will never fail.

FATHER, WHEN I CAN'T SLEEP, BRING YOUR MERCY AND COMPASSION TO MY MIND. GIVE ME HOPE IN YOUR FAITHFULNESS. THANK YOU FOR THE PROMISE OF THE NEW MORNING, AND HELP ME TO REST IN YOU. AMEN.

Delightfully You

*You [Judah] shall no more be termed Forsaken,
nor shall your land be called Desolate any more.
But you shall be called Hephzibah [My delight is
in her], and your land be called Beulah [married];
for the Lord delights in you, and your land shall be
married [owned and protected by the Lord].*

Isaiah 62:4 AMPC

Your name at birth is the first gift from your parents *and* your first identity. But no matter how you have been labeled until now, your God has given you a new name.

The terms *forsaken* and *desolate* call forth images of a dry, deserted barren land where nothing grows or flourishes. But "My Delight" is the new name God gives you. Captivated by you, He adores spending time with you. He awakens you with a brilliant sunrise and lulls you to sleep with a glowing moon and twinkling stars, heavenly displays that show how much pleasure He takes in you.

Let go of the other names you have accumulated: Too Heavy, Too Tall, Not Smart Enough, Not Pretty Enough, Too Much Trouble. You *are* enough. . .and not too much. God is not seeking perfection, beauty, or grace. He is seeking *you*. Bloom in the love of a Father who has renamed you His Delight.

FATHER GOD, THANK YOU FOR DELIGHTING IN ME. HELP ME TO FULLY ACCEPT MY NEW NAME AND LIVE AS ONE ACCEPTED AND ADORED BY HER FATHER. AMEN.

Mercy Will Be There

But you, beloved, building yourselves up on your most holy faith, praying in the Holy Spirit, keep yourselves in the love of God, looking for the mercy of our Lord Jesus Christ unto eternal life.

JUDE 20–21 NKJV

Do you have a lot on your mind today—worries about what's coming in the future? Take encouragement from Jude. In his letter, after his warnings to readers about apostate teachers in the church, Jude encouraged his readers to persevere in the faith despite their great trouble. He instructed them to follow this pattern: Turning away from your "mere natural instincts" (verse 19 NIV), stop focusing on yourselves and look toward God, from whom comes all good; look for Christ's mercy actively and expectantly, for He will keep you eternally.

No matter the danger you see ahead or the worst-case scenarios that leave you trembling, Christ's mercy will be there. The one who promised is faithful. Ask yourself: In your starkest imaginings, how could God's mercy show up? Then look for it—*expect* it—to show up in your life, doing so in the Spirit, submerging yourself in God's love, enriching your faith. And trust Him to be merciful to you as you strive toward the good.

JESUS, YOUR GOODNESS AND MERCY WILL FOLLOW HARD AFTER ME ALL THE DAYS OF MY LIFE, FOR YOU ARE GOOD AND PERFECTLY FAITHFUL—WHEN FEAR HITS, HELP ME TO BE LOOKING FOR HOW YOUR MERCY WILL SHOW UP.

Replacing Worry

Don't fret or worry. Instead of worrying, pray. Let petitions and praises shape your worries into prayers, letting God know your concerns. Before you know it, a sense of God's wholeness, everything coming together for good, will come and settle you down. It's wonderful what happens when Christ displaces worry at the center of your life.

PHILIPPIANS 4:6–7 MSG

Has worry made a home in your heart? Are you so used to stomach-knotting fretting tied to anxious thoughts that getting rid of it seems impossible? Are you concerned that if you extracted worry from your life, it may actually leave a hole in your heart?

Our Father, in His unending compassion for our hearts and spirits, gives us a perfect replacement for worry: prayer.

When you replace worry with prayer, God's Word promises you not just an absence of anxiety and fear but the *addition* of peace. Telling Him about your concerns brings the peace of Christ that goes beyond any understanding or rational explanation. Praising Him for what He has done in the past and clinging to the hope of what He's doing now and in your future brings wholeness that can only come from God's perfect plan. Prayer brings rest, contentment, safety, security, and confidence only found in the Savior, Jesus Christ.

Want to worry less? Then pray more!

WORRY HAS NO HOME IN THIS HEART ANYMORE, FATHER. TAKE AWAY MY ANXIOUS THOUGHTS AND ASSURE ME THAT YOU ARE NEAR. WHEN WORRIES TRY TO CREEP BACK, REPLACE THEM WITH THE PEACE OF CHRIST.

Just Half a Cup

"I am coming to you now, but I say these things while I am still in the world, so that they may have the full measure of my joy within them."

John 17:13 niv

"Just half a cup, please." You offer a friend a cup of piping hot coffee, but she declines a full cup, accepting only a small amount. Perhaps she is trying to be polite, or maybe she feels as though she's had enough coffee already that day. But it is difficult and unnatural for you to stop pouring at half a cup, so you pour just a bit more than what was requested. You want to give your friend the fullest possible measure of enjoyment that she can in that one cup of coffee.

That's how our Father feels when He longs to bestow His richest blessings and wisdom on us. He loves us, so He desires to fill our cups to overflowing with the things that He knows will bring us pleasure and growth. Do you tell Him to stop pouring when your cup is only half full? You may not even realize it, but perhaps your actions dictate that your cup remains half empty. Seek a full cup and enjoy the full measure of the joy of the Lord.

DEAR JESUS, FORGIVE ME FOR NOT ACCEPTING THE FULLNESS OF YOUR BLESSINGS AND YOUR JOY. HELP ME TO SEE THE WAYS THAT I PREVENT MY CUP FROM BEING FILLED TO OVERFLOWING. THANK YOU FOR WANTING ME TO HAVE THE FULLNESS OF YOUR JOY. AMEN.

My Morning Prayer

Let me hear Your faithfulness in the morning, for I trust in You; teach me the way in which I should walk; for to You I lift up my soul.

Psalm 143:8 nasb

Do mornings excite or depress you? When David wrote Psalm 143, he probably dreaded the sun coming up because that meant his enemies could continue pursuing him and persecuting his soul. "The enemy. . .has crushed my life to the ground" (verse 3 nasb). "My spirit feels weak within me; my heart is appalled" (verse 4).

What did David do when he didn't know which way to go? He turned to the Lord. He stayed in prayer with God and meditated on God's faithfulness and righteousness (verse 1), God's past work in his life (verse 5), and His loyal love (verses 8, 12). He also took refuge in God (verse 9) and continued serving Him (verse 12).

No matter what our day holds, we can face it confidently by practicing verse 8. Let's look for God's loving-kindness and keep trusting Him no matter what. Let's ask Him to teach and lead us in the way He wants us to go. We have the privilege of offering up our souls (thoughts, emotions, and will) to Him anew each morning. We can have a good day.

GOOD MORNING, LORD. YOU ARE MY LOVING FATHER, SECURE REFUGE, AND TRUSTWORTHY GOD. DELIVER ME FROM MY ENEMIES AND SHOW ME YOUR LOVING HEART AS I TRUST IN YOU. HELP ME TO PLEASE YOU TODAY IN MY DECISIONS AND GOALS, IN MY ATTITUDES TOWARD MY CIRCUMSTANCES, AND IN THE WAY I RESPOND TO THE PEOPLE AROUND ME.

God's Gift: Power, Love, and a Sound Mind

For God has not given us a spirit of fear,
but of power and of love and of a sound mind.
2 TIMOTHY 1:7 NKJV

Have you ever been completely surprised and delighted by a present? God the Father has given each believer the amazing gift of His Spirit. This gift is too immense to wrap yet lives inside you so that you are never without it.

God has gifted you a spirit of *power*, for He knows you will have many battles to fight. You will need to endure hard times. You may need to defend yourself against those who would want you to think you are less than you are. Using your spirit of power for good will only confirm your courage.

God has given you a spirit of *love*. This gift whispers of endurance, grace, and even boldness. To love boldly despite past hurts isn't easy. But God's love triumphs over all obstacles. So don't be afraid to love others and yourself with abandonment.

A *sound mind* is a gift that is well balanced and keeps all things in calm perspective. When the chaos of the day begins to swirl around you, breathe deeply and remember you have the sound mind of Christ. It's steady and able to accurately prioritize the steps needed for you to flourish.

FATHER GOD, I'M IN AWE OF YOUR SPIRIT WITHIN ME. THANK YOU FOR YOUR AMAZING GIFT! LET POWER, LOVE, AND A SOUND MIND BE MY WATCHWORDS EVERY DAY.

Transformation Proclamation

Sing to the Lord, all the earth! Tell of his salvation from day to day. Declare his glory among the nations, his marvelous works among all the peoples! For great is the Lord, and greatly to be praised, and he is to be feared above all gods.

1 Chronicles 16:23–25 ESV

Have you noticed a difference in your thought life or a change in your overall attitude since you became a believer? Chances are you have witnessed some improvements. Or maybe someone has told you she sees a change in you. Maybe certain situations just don't have the same effect on you as they once did.

Even so, when going through tests or trials, you may be tempted to entertain negative thoughts or adopt a bad attitude. If that happens, if your old ways begin to rise up in your heart and mind, rest assured that God sees you, and He understands! He has compassion for you. And because of that compassion, He has a word for you, a scripture verse or a prayer, a transformation proclamation that you can write down, one that reminds you that you're a new creation. That the old way of thinking and reacting is gone. That you have been transformed by the renewing of your mind.

LORD, YOU ARE THE GREAT EQUIPPER. AS I READ YOUR WORD, YOU TRANSFORM MY MIND AND ATTITUDE. AS I PRAY, LOOK UPON ME WITH COMPASSION. LEAD ME OUT OF ALL DARKNESS AND INTO YOUR LIGHT.

A Hiding Place

God is good, a hiding place in tough times. He recognizes and welcomes anyone looking for help, no matter how desperate the trouble.

Nahum 1:7–8 MSG

Think about some of the most troublesome things in your life. What do you stress over and worry about the most?

- Your health?
- Your finances?
- Your relationships?
- Your career?
- Your family?
- Or something else?

No matter what troubles you may encounter in this life—big or small—remember that in all of it, God is good. He is compassionate and kind. And in the uttermost darkness, God is your light. He protects His children—and that's a promise you can count on! With Him in your life, you can overcome any hardship. The Bible says to "Give all your worries and cares to God, for he cares about you" (1 Peter 5:7 NLT) and "Don't be discouraged, for I am your God. I will strengthen you and help you. I will hold you up with my victorious right hand" (Isaiah 41:10 NLT).

Isn't it wonderful? God recognizes what you're going through—*and* what's more, He's standing by, ready to offer His help. In fact, He *welcomes* you and all your troubles. So hand over your worries and cares to Him today—and then be sure to thank Him for His unending goodness!

GOD, YOU ARE SO, SO GOOD.

Taking a Real Sabbath

By the seventh day God had finished the work he had been doing; so on the seventh day he rested from all his work.
GENESIS 2:2 NIV

One of the Ten Commandments is to honor the Sabbath and keep it holy. God gives the example we can follow. In Genesis 2, He rested after His work was done.

What does honoring the Sabbath look like for women today? Some churches practice a literal Sabbath on Saturday and others take Sunday as their day of rest. Some Sabbath-keeping women rest from shopping and cooking, and many women who have to work on Sunday take another day as their personal Sabbath.

But too often we let our Sabbath day become as packed as the other six. We rush to get ready for church, then sing in the praise team, teach Sunday school, and (whew!) go to a meeting over lunch. The afternoon is for running errands, and the evening is spent in a discipleship group.

All those activities are fine in themselves. But when we overextend ourselves every single day, we run the risk of burning out—and forgetting why God created the Sabbath. He did it not so we could have another commandment to keep, but for our own good. Our bodies, minds, and emotions need rest. The Sabbath gives us a chance to take a breather. As we slow down our schedules and quiet our hearts, we can more easily hear from Him.

GOD, FORGIVE ME FOR TAKING YOUR COMMANDS TOO LIGHTLY. HELP ME TO REMEMBER THE SABBATH AND KEEP IT HOLY, JUST AS YOU DID.

This Is the Day That the Lord Has Made

This is the day which the Lord *has made;*
let's rejoice and be glad in it.
Psalm 118:24 NASB

Have you ever wondered how a perfectly good day can get so messed up?

The answer can usually be laid down to human behavior. All it takes is a sharp word to a family member or an unhelpful attitude or an unkind action and the situation quickly degenerates. Personal failure has odd tentacles. The guilty feeling from knowing the problem was self-instigated fosters a desire to shift the blame and then in the end leads to self-incriminating despair again being the cause of strife.

Human relationships, while having the strength to withstand much trauma, are remarkably fragile when it comes to insult. Our friends and husbands and children can be hurt greatly when we are careless with our words and attitudes. So how do we fix the day?

We can turn to our God, who is the essence of redemption. Since He sent Jesus to redeem our souls, He is able also to redeem even the smallest earthly concern. Coming to Him for mercy is the first step in righting the wrong. Exchanging our failures for His grace reminds us that all is not lost. The day is His, after all, and He offers the hope we need to live it through to the end.

FATHER GOD, THANK YOU FOR YOUR ABUNDANT MERCY AND CONSTANT GRACE. REDEEM MY FAILURES TODAY AND HELP ME NOT TO REPEAT THEM. IN JESUS' NAME, AMEN.

Present and Future Hope

Therefore, with minds that are alert and fully sober, set your hope on the grace to be brought to you when Jesus Christ is revealed at his coming.

1 PETER 1:13 NIV

Your hope is both a present down payment and a future possession. Waiting for "the gift that's coming when Jesus arrives" (1:13 MSG), you act like a child at Christmas, quick to notice anything unusual in your surroundings, whether reindeer and jingle bells. . .or a whisper of the Holy Spirit.

To fully appreciate this hope, you must remain sober, serious, and dedicated to the task at hand. You are holding your breath, not blinking.

Like an anchor, your hope goes deep and takes hold, grounded in grace that will come. Nothing can move you off course. When Christ returns, grace will complete your transformation into Christlikeness, and you will be resurrected with an imperishable body (see 1 Corinthians 15:42).

You are able to grab ahold of that future hope of God's grace because of what it has already done. Your salvation is a completed act; you already have the eternal life that you will enter more fully when you reach heaven.

ETERNAL GOD, LET ME LIVE IN LIGHT OF YOUR GRACE THAT SUSTAINS ME IN THE PRESENT AND GIVES ME HOPE FOR THE FUTURE.

Imprint It

His work is honorable and glorious, and His righteousness endures forever. He has made His wonderful works to be remembered; the Lord is gracious, merciful, and full of loving compassion. He has given food and provision to those who reverently and worshipfully fear Him; He will remember His covenant forever and imprint it [on His mind].

PSALM 111:3–5 AMPC

The Bible contains many promises. As a woman of God, consider all the promises He made to you and followed through on over the past few years. Doing so will help you to realize the strength found in knowing that no matter how good or challenging life might get, God always keeps His promises to you.

In the verses above, the word *imprint* stands out. To imprint is to impress, produce, or fix firmly on the mind in memory. Here God is telling you, reminding you, that He will never forget His promises—to always be with you, go before you, love you, bless you, and so much more.

So if there are moments you forget God's promises, waver in your faith, or feel like you just don't know what to do next, take heart in knowing that God has never forgotten you! And that His promises are there for the taking. Imprint them on your mind and heart, and you'll find your life, your very self, transformed.

LORD, HELP ME REMEMBER YOUR WORDS. TRANSFORM ME BY IMPRESSING YOUR PROMISES IN MY MIND AND ON MY HEART.

Respite

The LORD said to Moses, "Speak to the Israelites and say to them: 'These are my appointed festivals, the appointed festivals of the LORD, which you are to proclaim as sacred assemblies. There are six days when you may work, but the seventh day is a day of sabbath rest, a day of sacred assembly. You are not to do any work; wherever you live, it is a sabbath to the LORD.'"

LEVITICUS 23:1–3 NIV

Through Moses, the Lord gave His people a solid foundation on which they can live a balanced life. This structure permits you six days in which to work, but declares that on the seventh day, you should rest, for your well-being. It is a respite from everyday life and gives you a chance to slow things down from earthly activity.

In this fast-paced world, it is important to take some time for yourself and to give thanks to God for His many blessings. How wonderful that you can hit PAUSE on the remote control of your life and enjoy some quiet time with Him. Through God's grace, you have the foundation for a well-lived, balanced life. Empowered through God's perfect structure, you can be the best you can be.

DEAR LORD, HELP ME STRUCTURE MY LIFE BASED ON YOUR UNSHAKABLE FOUNDATION CREATED JUST FOR ME. THANK YOU FOR CONSIDERING MY EVERY NEED, BOTH SPIRITUAL AND PHYSICAL, AND FOR THIS DAY OF REST. AMEN.

The Practice of Praise

Bless the Lord, *O my soul: and all that is within me. . . . Bless the* Lord, *O my soul, and forget not all his benefits: who forgiveth all thine iniquities; who healeth all thy diseases; who redeemeth thy life from destruction.*

Psalm 103:1–4 kjv

Trials come to all of us, and when they do, it's easy to forget all that God has done for us in the past. Often our adverse circumstances sabotage our efforts to praise God in every situation.

The psalmist practiced the power of praise as he acknowledged God's faithfulness to forgive, heal, and restore. He blessed the Lord with his whole heart because he trusted in God's divine plan.

Positive acclamations of our faith produce remarkable results. First, praise establishes and builds our faith. It decrees, "No matter what is happening, no matter how I feel, I choose to praise God!" Second, praise changes our perspective. As we relinquish control, praise redirects our focus toward God rather than on our problems. And third, praise blesses the heart of God. It brings God joy for His children to acknowledge His presence and power through praise.

The Bible admonishes us to praise God in every circumstance, saying, "In every thing give thanks: for this is the will of God in Christ Jesus concerning you" (1 Thessalonians 5:18 kjv). To bless the Lord in all things is to receive God's blessings. Begin the practice of praise today!

HEAVENLY FATHER, YOU ARE WORTHY OF ALL MY PRAISE. I THANK AND PRAISE YOU FOR MY CURRENT CIRCUMSTANCES, KNOWING THAT YOU ARE AT WORK ON MY BEHALF. AMEN.

Praise and Thanksgiving

Enter his gates with thanksgiving and his courts with praise; give thanks to him and praise his name.

Psalm 100:4 NIV

In Old Testament times, the people went to the temple to meet with God. God's presence resided there just once a year after the sacrifice had been made on the Day of Atonement. But people came many times a year for festivals and to offer sacrifices for sin. The gates were the entrance to the temple grounds. And through the gates were the courts. They were the outside area where the people gathered. Part of this area was dedicated to altars for sacrifices.

Now that God lives within us through His Holy Spirit, we don't have to go to a temple or church to find Him. He is always with us. How then should this verse impact our relationship with God now? When we go to Him in prayer, let's consider starting with thanksgiving and moving into praise. Thanksgiving is thanking God for what He has done for us and how He has provided for us. Praise is identifying and acknowledging the characteristics of God, such as Creator, healer, righteous, merciful, loving.

We are commanded to give thanks and praise God's name. As we do so, our worries, fears, confessions, and requests fall into their proper place.

HEAVENLY FATHER, THANK YOU THAT WE CAN WORSHIP YOU WITHOUT GOING TO A BUILDING. YOU ARE ALWAYS WITH US. WE PRAISE YOU FOR YOUR MERCY IN MAKING A WAY FOR US TO HAVE A RELATIONSHIP WITH YOU. REMIND US OF WHO YOU ARE AND HELP US TO CLING TO YOU. AMEN.

High and Wide

"The Lord our God is merciful and forgiving, even though we have rebelled against him."
DANIEL 9:9 NIV

In Daniel 9, Daniel comes before God in sackcloth and ashes, mourning his sin and the sins of Israel. With great humility, he confesses the nation's transgressions, pleading with God to turn away from His righteous anger. Daniel even fasted, depriving himself of food to show his devotion and sincerity.

Does this radical display of repentance make you squirm a little? When was the last time you approached God with a similar level of remorse for your sin and with the same drive for change and transformation in your life? In a society where sin is often downplayed or viewed as the norm, simply shrugging off your sin and shrinking it down to a speck in your mind's eye is easy.

Your view of sin directly affects your view of God's grace. If you believe your sins to be slight, then your perception of God's grace will also be small by comparison. However, if you acknowledge the magnitude and weight of your iniquities, you will come to realize just how high and wide God's grace stretches to wash them clean. As Daniel affirms, the Lord is merciful and forgiving, despite all your rebellion.

THANK YOU, LORD GOD, FOR COVERING ALL OF MY SINS, EVERY LAST ONE. IMPRINT THIS TRUTH ON MY HEART AND MAKE IT FRESH EACH MORNING.

Finding Your Way Back

Manasseh sought the LORD his God and sincerely humbled himself before the God of his ancestors. And when he prayed, the LORD listened to him and was moved by his request.

2 CHRONICLES 33:12–13 NLT

When Hezekiah died, his son Manasseh became king of Judah. But he followed idols, built up the high places where he burned his children as sacrifices, and made altars to worship foreign gods—in God's house! And his people followed his reckless behavior.

God tried to turn His people around, to bring them back to Him, but they wouldn't listen. So God allowed Assyria to take Manasseh prisoner. "They put a ring through his nose, bound him in bronze chains, and led him away to Babylon" (2 Chronicles 33:11 NLT).

That's when Manasseh prayed to God who, in His compassion, listened to the king and brought him back to Jerusalem. That's when "Manasseh finally realized that the LORD alone is God!" (2 Chronicles 33:13 NLT).

No matter what you've done, if you sincerely repent (turn around), if you change and come back to God, you can move the one who moves the world.

Consider where God may be speaking into *your* life, where He may be wanting you to change. Then pray, knowing that God is listening and, if you're sincere, that He will be moved by your plea—and will bring you back home to Him, where you belong.

GOD, OPEN MY EARS TO YOUR VOICE.
HELP ME FIND MY WAY BACK HOME TO YOU.

True Strength

That is why, for Christ's sake, I delight in weaknesses, in insults, in hardships, in persecutions, in difficulties. For when I am weak, then I am strong.

2 CORINTHIANS 12:10 NIV

Everyone has tough days. Sometimes they expand into weeks, months, or years of trial.

The apostle Paul was given a thorn in his flesh. Although it's not known exactly what his malady was, he did plead with Jesus to remove that thorn. That's when Jesus told him, "My grace is enough; it's all you need. My strength comes into its own in your weakness" (2 Corinthians 12:9 MSG).

Those words turned Paul's life, his view of his weakness and hardships, around! Paul wrote, "Once I heard that, I was glad to let it happen. I quit focusing on the handicap and began appreciating the gift. It was a case of Christ's strength moving in on my weakness" (2 Corinthians 12:9 MSG).

Just like Paul, you too can learn how to "take limitations in stride, and with good cheer" (2 Corinthians 12:10 MSG). When you feel as if you can't go on, when weakness threatens to overtake you, simply allow Christ to take over. For the weaker you get, the stronger you will become through Him.

DEAR GOD, HELP ME TURN AROUND MY VIEW OF MY WEAKNESSES AND HARDSHIPS. INSTEAD OF ALLOWING THEM TO BRING ME DOWN, HELP ME DELIGHT IN THEM. HELP ME FACE ALL THINGS WITH YOUR GRACE. AND IN JESUS' NAME. FOR HE IS MY TRUE STRENGTH. AMEN.

A Refuge from Our Despair

Hear my cry, God; give Your attention to my prayer.
From the end of the earth I call to You when my heart
is faint; lead me to the rock that is higher than I.
For You have been a refuge for me, a tower of strength
against the enemy. Let me dwell in Your tent forever;
let me take refuge in the shelter of Your wings.
PSALM 61:1–4 NASB

King David, writer of this psalm, composed it as a song, acknowledging God as his rock. He clung with tenacity to the fact that no matter how desperate his situation appeared, God was as immovable as a huge rock or boulder. Although David's trials may differ from yours, you too can use strong coping mechanisms.

First, David acknowledged God remained all powerful, despite life circumstances. And second, David looked back at God's past rescues. "My soul is in despair within me; therefore I remember You from the land of the Jordan and the peaks of Hermon, from Mount Mizar. Deep calls to deep at the sound of Your waterfalls; all Your breakers and Your waves have passed over me. The LORD will send His goodness in the daytime; and His song will be with me in the night, a prayer to the God of my life" (Psalm 42:6-8 NASB).

LORD, I SEARCH FOR A WAY THROUGH THE TORRENTS OF DESPAIR. HOW PRECIOUS IS THE KNOWLEDGE THAT YOU HEAR AND CARE.

No Shame

Those who look to him for help will be radiant with joy; no shadow of shame will darken their faces.

Psalm 34:5 NLT

Adam and Eve had the perfect home—a beautiful garden. Every plant, tree, and animal was theirs. Their perfect Father met every one of their needs. His rules were clear. All the garden belonged to them—except the fruit of the one tree. Adam was told plainly by God: Eat the fruit of this tree, and you will surely die (Genesis 2:16–17).

Of course, the one thing they couldn't have was the one thing that captured their attention. When the serpent presented an opportunity, Adam and Eve took the bait. What followed was a feeling known to all of us thereafter—shame. They hid their faces and their bodies from God, covered with the profound awareness that they had failed Him. In the cool of the garden, Adam tried to avoid God and hide from Him further. Yes, the consequences were severe, but God demanded Adam and Eve look to Him so He could remove their shame.

No matter how we disappoint God, we never have to hide from Him or cover our faces in shame. All we need to do is turn to Him and ask for His forgiveness, mercy, and grace. One look at the Father, and our faces can be radiant with joy.

FATHER, WHEN I HAVE DISAPPOINTED YOU, THE LAST THING I WANT IS TO LOOK TO YOU FOR HELP. I KNOW IT'S BECAUSE I CAN'T COMPREHEND YOUR MERCY AND YOUR LOVE FOR ME. THANK YOU FOR FREEDOM FROM THE SHADOW OF SHAME. AMEN.

When All the World Falls Apart

The Sovereign LORD is my strength; he makes my feet like the feet of a deer, he enables me to tread on the heights.

HABAKKUK 3:19 NIV

Ever feel like the moment you get one part of your life put together and looking good, another part falls into bits?

That's the bitter effects of living in a fallen world. And the way of all humanity. Yes, some people seem to have an easier time of it than others. Yet if they live long enough, trouble will come. Whether it's a bad report from the doctor, a beloved friendship broken off, a financial crisis, a prodigal child, an unforgiving spouse, a stress-filled work environment, a flooded home, or a betrayal within the church. . .trouble seems to hound humanity relentlessly.

But thank God there is hope amid your many trials. In Habakkuk you can see that even though the hour of trouble may come, the Lord is your strength. He will not only lift you up but give you a lightness of spirit. Just like the deer. If you have ever watched a deer leap through the woods, you know that amazing nimbleness, that graceful soaring in action.

And that strength and lightness are what God offers you. Rest in that knowledge. Call on the Lord, knowing His promise is meant not only for the whole world but for you specifically.

HOLY SPIRIT, DWELL IN ME FULLY, SO THAT WHEN TROUBLE COMES, I MIGHT KNOW YOUR STRENGTH. AMEN.

Watching Over

The Lord watches over the foreigner and sustains the fatherless and the widow, but he frustrates the ways of the wicked.

Psalm 146:9 NIV

Lost. Abandoned. Neglected. Forgotten. There are times in each of our lives when we may have these feelings. And we don't have to be a refugee or an orphan or have lost a husband to feel lonely. But because we do feel these ways, we should be able to imagine all the more what it must be like to be in a position in which we have suddenly lost everything that makes home feel like home and all the things that are familiar and bring comfort. And we should then be able to have compassion for those who are in such a position.

Yet our gentle, loving, ever-present Father God transforms us. He watches over us and cares for us and provides for us. In His love, we are changed—those who are lost are found. Those who are fatherless are welcomed into Daddy's arms. Those with broken hearts are made whole again. God's love is powerful and surprising—showing up in some of the most mysterious places. And every time we are met with unconditional love, with unmerited favor, with generous gifts of grace, we can know that we are experiencing the love of our perfect Father.

LORD, THANK YOU FOR YOUR GENTLE LOVE THAT MAKES ME YOUR CHILD. AMEN.

A Generous and Gracious Lord

Oh, how generous and gracious our Lord was! He filled me with the faith and love that come from Christ Jesus.

1 TIMOTHY 1:14 NLT

In his letter to Timothy, the apostle Paul reminds us of his storied past. Before his encounter with Jesus in Acts 9, Paul was raised to be a zealous Pharisee like his father (Acts 23:6). His Jewish heritage, discipline, and passion were unmatched (Philippians 3:4–6). He hated and actively persecuted Christians. He had active roles in their deaths and imprisonments (Acts 8:1).

Yet because of God's love and compassion, Paul was forgiven much, and he knew his story was a beautiful example of the saving grace of the Father—of the transforming power of God's love. If God saved this man with such a wicked heart full of evil *and* God trusted Paul to be a messenger of Christ, then God can do the same for you too.

Today, let go of the guilt of your past. God is ready and willing to forgive and accept you. God forgave Paul and used Paul mightily for His kingdom. God can and will use you mightily too!

FATHER GOD, TODAY I'M RELEASING THE SHAME OF MY PAST. I'M LIFTING MY EYES TO YOU AND ASKING FOR FORGIVENESS AND FREEDOM FROM THE GUILT I'VE FELT FOR SO LONG. RAISE ME UP AND REMIND ME THAT I'M YOUR CHERISHED DAUGHTER WHO CAN AND WILL BE INVOLVED IN MIGHTY THINGS IN YOUR KINGDOM.

He Enjoys You

The LORD *your God is in your midst, a mighty one who will save; he will rejoice over you with gladness; he will quiet you by his love; he will exult over you with loud singing.*

ZEPHANIAH 3:17 ESV

Memory is a powerful part of each one of us. Perhaps you can see your father cheering you on in a sports event or you remember your mother stroking your feverish forehead while you lay sick in bed. With those mental pictures comes a recollection of emotion—how good it felt to be cheered and encouraged—how comforting it was to be loved and attended to.

Zephaniah's words remind us that God is our loving parent. Our mighty Savior offers us a personal relationship, loving and rejoicing over us His children, glad that we live and move in Him. He is the Lord of the universe, and yet He will quiet our restless hearts and minds with His tender love. He delights in our lives and celebrates our union with Him. We can rest in His affirmation and love, no matter what circumstances surround us.

LORD, HELP ME REMEMBER THAT YOU ARE ALWAYS WITH ME AND THAT YOU DELIGHT IN ME. REMIND ME THAT I AM YOUR CHILD AND THAT YOU ENJOY OUR RELATIONSHIP.

Draw Near with Confidence

Therefore let's approach the throne of grace with confidence, so that we may receive mercy and find grace for help at the time of our need.

Hebrews 4:16 NASB

In this verse you are told that you can approach God's throne with confidence. Why do you approach the throne? So that you can receive mercy and find grace to help in time of need. Why would you need to receive mercy? Those who need mercy are those who have done something wrong, those who are not in right standing with whomever they are asking mercy from. Inevitably you come before the throne of God with the baggage of your sin. And yet you are told to come with confidence before the throne of a holy God who hates sin. You don't need to be perfect or have your act together to come before God with confidence. You only need to be covered in Christ's blood. This confidence with which you approach God's throne is not a self-confidence, but a God-confidence. It's a confidence that assures you that God is for you, that He loves you, and that He sees Christ in you. Your standing before God depends completely on His view of you and not on your own merit. And He sees you as His beloved child. So go boldly to the foot of His throne, knowing that you will receive mercy and grace.

LORD, THANK YOU THAT I DON'T NEED TO BE PERFECT BEFORE I CAN COME BEFORE YOU. I COME BEFORE YOU NOW WITH MY CONFIDENCE PLACED IN YOU, NOT IN MY OWN MERIT.

A Daily Walk with God

And they heard the sound of the Lord God walking in the garden in the cool of the day, and Adam and his wife hid themselves from the presence of the Lord God among the trees of the garden. But the Lord God called to Adam and said to him, Where are you?

Genesis 3:8–9 AMPC

Are you an on-time person, or are you constantly running late? Does the tardiness of others or your own put a strain on your friendships? Imagine what it would be like to have an appointment with God every day. Time allotted not to do anything in particular, but simply to spend time with Him, sharing your heart in conversation and companionship.

That must have been what it was like in those early days of Eden. How did Adam and Eve feel knowing God would come down from heaven just to spend time with them? Were they excited to see Him, or did they take His presence for granted?

You can experience God each day. He desires to spend time with you. He wants you, His child, to share your heart with Him. Are you there, waiting to hear His voice? Abide in Him and talk with Him today.

GOD, FORGIVE ME FOR ALLOWING THE BUSYNESS OF LIFE TO CONSUME ME. REMIND ME THAT NOTHING IS MORE IMPORTANT THAN ABIDING IN YOU.

More Jesus

"Are you tired? Worn out? Burned out on religion? Come to me. Get away with me and you'll recover your life. I'll show you how to take a real rest. Walk with me and work with me—watch how I do it. Learn the unforced rhythms of grace. I won't lay anything heavy or ill-fitting on you. Keep company with me and you'll learn to live freely and lightly."

MATTHEW 11:28–30 MSG

When was the last time you had a real, honest-to-goodness rest? The kind that refreshes you both mentally and physically, that makes you feel completely revitalized and alive?

If that sounds like wishful thinking. . .if your mind tells you, *Yeah, right! I haven't had a good rest in at least ten years—and there's no end in sight for me!* . . .take these words from Matthew 11 to heart. Jesus says, "Get away with me. . . . I'll show you how to take a real rest." What a promise!

Instead of more *busy* in your life, get more of *Jesus.* He is just what your weary soul needs. He will pull you from the depths of your day-to-day burnout and give you rest like you've never experienced it before—a rest that leads to free and light living! Praise Him!

FATHER GOD, REST GIVER, COMFORT MY WORLD-WEARY SOUL TODAY. I AM EXHAUSTED! I TRUST YOU TO SHOW ME THE WAY TO REFRESHING REST. THANK YOU!

Great Goodness

How great is Your goodness that You have stored up for those who fear You and. . .for those who take refuge in You. You hide them in the protection of Your presence; You conceal them in a shelter from the schemes of men. . . . Love the L*ORD*, *all His faithful ones. . . . Be strong and courageous, all you who put your hope in the* L*ORD*.

PSALM 31:19–20, 23–24 HCSB

When you're up against it, where do you turn? When you see no way out, where do you go? When you are like a city under siege, who do you cry to? No matter how far down you are, there's someone waiting to grasp your hand, to pour blessings upon you, to provide you with shelter. And that one person is God.

When you trust in God, He'll do anything to rescue you, protect you, and provide for you. The schemes others work against you will come to nothing. When you feel you've lost sight of His light, when you cry out to Him, pleading to Him for help and mercy, He'll hear you. He'll move into action. He'll part the seas, stop the sun, and still the waves.

And what does God ask in return? That you love, obey, trust in, and follow Him. So, dear friend, be strong. Be brave. And put all your trust and hope in God. He will never fail you.

I LOVE YOU, LORD. BE MY REFUGE, MY STRENGTH, MY HOPE, AND MY HEART. AMEN.

Jesus, the Good Shepherd

"But the one who enters by the door is a shepherd of the sheep.
To him the doorkeeper opens, and the sheep listen to his voice,
and he calls his own sheep by name and leads them out."

JOHN 10:2–3 NASB

Sheep just aren't very bright. They need constant overseeing, tender treatment, and strict boundaries. The shepherd took them to the best pastures, found safe lodging for them during the night, and then led them out again in the morning. He was the ultimate caregiver!

In fact, the shepherd would stretch his own body out across the opening to the sheep pen. What a graphic picture of protection this provides as we consider that Christ considers Himself our shepherd.

As the world screams out for us to follow every wind of doctrine, Christ's voice calls us back to obedience: "When he puts all his own sheep outside, he goes ahead of them, and the sheep follow him because they know his voice" (John 10:4 NASB). His voice will never call us to rebellion, sinful pleasures, or departure from His Word.

In our day we hear those who defend heinous acts by saying, "Voices told me to do it." Certainly, the one they chose to listen to was not the voice of Jesus Christ, for He cannot contradict Himself. True sheep listen only for the voice of their shepherd.

God calls us by name, just as the shepherd has pet names for his sheep. Someday, when the King of kings, our good shepherd, calls us home to heaven, we'll hear the names He calls us.

LORD, GUIDE ME TO SAFE PASTURES TODAY. NEVER LEAVE ME.

No More Tears

"'He will wipe every tear from their eyes. There will be no more death' or mourning or crying or pain, for the old order of things has passed away."
REVELATION 21:4 NIV

This world is sadly full of sorrow and disappointment. But God doesn't allow our pain to be purposeless. It helps us need Jesus more. It drives us to a closer, more dependent relationship with Him, even when we can't possibly understand the reason for the pain we are experiencing.

Pain, especially when it's seen in our rearview mirrors rather than in front of our faces, helps us have greater compassion for others' suffering. It also gives us common ground to give comfort and empathize with others who are in painful circumstances.

It won't always be like this. Someday we will live with Jesus in a perfect life with no sorrow, pain, or disappointment. And we have a "no more tears" promise that is greater than any baby shampoo could deliver. Someday we will have joy greater than anything this earth can offer because it won't be tainted by sin and death. And that is a promise we can hold on to.

HEAVENLY FATHER, THANK YOU SO MUCH FOR DEFEATING DEATH AND SIN SO WE CAN HAVE A GLORIOUS FUTURE WITH YOU IN HEAVEN, WHERE WE WILL TRULY HAVE NO MORE TEARS. HELP US TO CLING TO YOUR PROMISES AND TO COMFORT OTHERS WHO ARE GOING THROUGH PAINFUL SITUATIONS. AMEN.

Quiet Moments

The Lord is my shepherd; I shall not want. He makes me to lie down in green pastures; He leads me beside the still waters. He restores my soul. . . . Yea, though I walk through the valley of the shadow of death, I will fear no evil; for You are with me.

Psalm 23:1–4 NKJV

You live in a loud world. From the busy rush hour traffic to the constant noise from technology, it's easy to fill every moment to capacity with the sounds and activities of life. Emails, social media, texts, and phone calls constantly interrupt the tasks you have to do for yourself and others. It's easy to become distracted and perhaps too busy for the Lord.

If you are not intentional about spending time with God, before you know it, you will have become distant or will have detoured away from Him. You find your soul is hungry for His presence and peace.

God is calling you to reconnect. No matter where you are, when you recognize your need for Him, stop whatever you are doing and step away from others. Once you are alone with Him, establish a reconnection. Allow His presence to wash over you and restore your soul.

LORD, MY PEACE COMES FROM YOU. FORGIVE ME WHEN I BECOME TOO BUSY. WHEN LIFE BEGINS TO CONSUME ME, SPEAK TO MY HEART AND DRAW ME TO YOU. HELP ME TO DISCONNECT FROM THE BUSYNESS OF THIS WORLD AND RECONNECT TO THE PEACE OF YOURS.

A Little Longer

"But he answered and said to him, 'Sir, let it alone this year also, until I dig around it and fertilize it. And if it bears fruit, well. But if not, after that you can cut it down.'"

Luke 13:8–9 NKJV

An ordinary day had just begun as the man surveyed his garden. Yes! Over there, in that open spot, was the perfect place for a fig tree. He summoned his gardener, who planted the tree. But day after day the man checked the tree only to find—nothing! No figs ever graced the branches. Three years went by without any fruit, and finally the man grew tired of that barren fig tree. "Cut it down," he ordered. "It's just taking up space in the garden" (Luke 13:7 NLT). The gardener, however, was not ready to write off the figless fig tree. He said, "Sir, give it one more chance. Leave it another year" (Luke 13:8 NLT). With extra care, maybe the tree would bear fruit.

Aren't you glad that our Lord is like the gardener? If our lives resemble the barren fig tree, Jesus does not shout, "Cut it down!" He intercedes for us. He is patient toward us. He puts in the extra work to make us fruitful. Let's not resist His hand when He digs up the soil and pours His Word into our hearts.

LORD, I WAS DORMANT FOR MANY YEARS. THANK YOU FOR GRACE. THANK YOU FOR YOUR TENDER CARE.

Heavenly Eyes

God looks down from heaven on all mankind to see if there are any who understand, any who seek God.

Psalm 53:2 NIV

As a child, you likely remember your parents looking out for you, making sure you were safe and had all you needed. That is the role of a good parent. As a result, you felt safe and loved. There was no stress regarding how you would survive or where your next meal would come from. There was just the knowledge that your needs were covered. And if you needed help, all you had to do was find your parents, look up at them, and ask.

Now that you're all grown up, your parents may or may not be around. But your heavenly Father definitely is. He looks down from heaven on you, looking to see if you understand what He's doing in your life. He wants to see if you are seeking Him.

As God looks down from heaven, He wants you to know He has everything under control. All He asks is that you look to *Him* for all things. That you be faithful to Him, living your life in accordance with His teachings and striving to better understand His Word.

Today, look to God for what you may need (Psalm 121:1–2). And while you do so, remember God is looking down, watching over you.

DEAR GOD, LOOK DOWN ON ME AS I, IN TURN, LOOK UPWARD, SEEKING YOU AND WORKING TO BROADEN MY UNDERSTANDING OF YOU.

Lay It at the Cross

"Come to me, all you who are weary and burdened, and I will give you rest. Take my yoke upon you and learn from me. . .and you will find rest for your souls. For my yoke is easy and my burden is light."

MATTHEW 11:28–30 NIV

Does life sometimes get you down? Often when we experience difficulties that weigh us down, we hear the old adage "Lay it at the cross." But how do we lay our difficulties at the cross?

Jesus gives us step-by-step guidance in how to place our difficulties and burdens at the foot of the cross. First, He invites us to come to Him; those of us who are weary and burdened just need to approach Jesus in prayer. Second, He exchanges our heavy and burdensome loads with His easy and light load. Jesus gives us His yoke and encourages us to learn from Him. The word *yoke* refers to Christ's teachings, Jesus' way of living life. As we follow His teachings, we take His yoke in humility and gentleness, surrendering and submitting ourselves to His will and ways for our lives. Finally, we praise God for the rest He promises to provide us.

Do you have any difficulties in life, any burdens, worries, fears, relationship issues, finance troubles, or work problems that you need to "lay at the cross"? Jesus says, "Come."

LORD, THANK YOU FOR INVITING ME TO COME AND EXCHANGE MY HEAVY BURDEN FOR YOUR LIGHT BURDEN. I PRAISE YOU FOR THE REST YOU PROMISE ME. AMEN.

Peace Beyond Comprehension

Do not be anxious about anything, but in every situation, by prayer and petition, with thanksgiving, present your requests to God. And the peace of God, which transcends all understanding, will guard your hearts and your minds in Christ Jesus.

PHILIPPIANS 4:6–7 NIV

Within the first hours of the day, many of us can find opportunities to worry. But as we learn to take every situation to God, He exchanges our worries for His peace.

We come before God and bring Him our needs, knowing He is the only one who can grant our requests. And we are to do this with thanksgiving. When we remember all God has done for us and provided for us, the worries that cause us to focus on what we don't have slip away in the presence of our mighty God.

God has compassion on us and knows that we worry about many things. He tells us many times to come to Him. In 1 Peter 5:7 He tells us to give Him our cares. In Matthew 6:25–33 He tells us He will provide for us and meet our needs.

God promises that peace will permeate both our hearts, where our feelings can churn painfully, and our minds, where we can turn situations over endlessly. Along with giving us His peace, God takes our minds into protective custody, cutting off worries before they can enter.

LORD JESUS, THANK YOU FOR GIVING US YOUR SUPERNATURAL PEACE. REMIND US TO BRING ALL OF OUR CARES TO YOU AND TO THANK YOU FOR EVERYTHING YOU'VE DONE FOR US.

Glimpses of Goodness

Jesus came and told his disciples, "I have been given all authority in heaven and on earth. Therefore, go and make disciples of all the nations, baptizing them in the name of the Father and the Son and the Holy Spirit. Teach these new disciples to obey all the commands I have given you. And be sure of this: I am with you always."

Matthew 28:18–20 NLT

Jesus' disciples saw the bloodshed and the pain. . .but they also witnessed the resurrected body. How could it be? Is this what Jesus meant when He said He'd come back?

Have you ever thought about how you would have responded if you had witnessed Jesus in His resurrected state? Would you have had the faith to believe it was Him, or not? And if you had still been skeptical after seeing His scarred hands and feet, would you have been willing to accept His Great Commission?

Fortunately, none of those "ifs" really matter. Because Jesus said, "Blessed are those who believe without seeing" (John 20:29 NLT). That's how the Christian faith is. You come to believe you are saved by grace and forgiven of your sins. You put your faith, hope, and trust in an eternal Father who has an eternal plan for you. And although you don't get to see Jesus on this side of heaven, you do get to see glimpses of His goodness.

THANK YOU, LORD, FOR YOUR PROVISION OF BLESSING ME AND MY LIFE REGARDLESS OF WHAT-IFS!

Preserved

You who love the L*ORD, hate evil! He preserves the souls of His saints; He delivers them out of the hand of the wicked.*

PSALM 97:10 NKJV

Have you ever preserved a food product, such as by freezing jam, canning vegetables, or dehydrating meat? If so, then you understand the process of longevity. You've given a particular food a longer shelf (or refrigerator/freezer) life. By adding preservatives (or drying the product out) you've taken something that was destined to shortly die and transitioned it into a long-lasting state.

Did you realize that God longs to preserve not just your life, your family, and your relationships. . .but your very soul? He pours Himself out—like a holy preservative—and says, "Your shelf life just got a *lot* longer. You're going to live, not just in this life, but for all eternity." Wow!

Today, take some time to ponder where your life would be without the Lord. Would you still be here? Would you have hope and a future? What a radical difference your God makes!

FATHER, I'M SO GRATEFUL YOU'VE EXTENDED MY SHELF LIFE. I GET TO LIVE FOREVER WITH YOU. AND WHAT A SWEET PRESERVATIVE YOU'VE GIVEN ME, ONE SEASONED WITH FORGIVENESS, GRACE, JOY, AND SO MUCH MORE. THANK YOU, LORD, FOR PRESERVING MY SOUL. AMEN.

Faithful in the Storm

O LORD God of hosts, who is mighty as you are,
O LORD, with your faithfulness all around you? You rule
the raging of the sea; when its waves rise, you still them. . . .
The world and all that is in it, you have founded them.

PSALM 89:8–9, 11 ESV

Perhaps nothing in creation can make us feel smaller than nature in the fury of a storm. Winds topple trees. Floods engulf entire towns. Once-solid land slides away. Waves higher than buildings leave rubble in their wake. Normally, nature soothes us—think gentle rains, lulling waves, and grounding earth—but when the storms roll in? Nature shakes us. . .unless we keep our minds fixed on God.

As mighty as nature's power seems, God is mightier. He is the power that controls creation itself. The Bible tells us that God rules over the raging sea. He stills the waves. What's more, our mighty God, who founded everything that exists, radiates faithfulness. He will not leave us alone in the storm.

And that's as true of nature's storms as it is of life's storms. God is in charge of the raging seasons that threaten to overwhelm us. He can still the waves of rising fear. Nothing is mightier, nor is there anyone more faithful than He.

LORD, WITH SUCH AN ALMIGHTY GOD AS YOU IN MY LIFE, I HAVE NO REASON TO BE AFRAID. REMIND ME OF YOUR FAITHFULNESS WHEN STORMS THREATEN TO SHAKE ME.

Where to Look for God

"When we heard of it, our hearts melted in fear and everyone's courage failed because of you, for the Lord your God is God in heaven above and on the earth below."

Joshua 2:11 NIV

The people of Jericho had reason to be worried. They had seen evidence of God's strength and support of His children—and knew that Joshua planned to conquer Canaan. As residents of the key military fortress in the land, they understood that Joshua would soon be at their gates.

Yet only Rahab seemed to recognize the right course of action: to embrace the Lord and open her home to Joshua's agents. In return, they made sure she and her family survived the attack. Because of her courage and faith, Rahab became an ancestress of Jesus.

Sometimes when our own lives seem to be under siege from the demands of work, bills, family, whatever—finding the work of God amid the strife can be difficult. Even though we acknowledge His power, we may overlook the gentle touches, the small ways in which He makes every day a little easier. Just as the Lord cares for the tiniest bird, so He seeks to be a part of every detail in your life (Matthew 10:29–31). Look for Him there.

FATHER GOD, I KNOW YOU ARE BY MY SIDE EVERY DAY, GOOD OR BAD, AND THAT YOU LOVE AND CARE FOR ME. HELP ME TO SEE YOUR WORK IN MY LIFE AND IN THE LIVES OF MY FRIENDS AND FAMILY.

Remembering His Promises

Tell everyone about God's power. His majesty shines down on Israel; his strength is mighty in the heavens. God is awesome in his sanctuary. The God of Israel gives power and strength to his people. Praise be to God!

PSALM 68:34–35 NLT

Do you ever find yourself dreaming of a place of safety? A place where you can close your eyes, rest your head, and let go of the stress and angst that follow you around like a shadow? It rarely matters what kind of season you are in—busy or calm—you always seem to feel an inner longing to find a place where there is nothing but peace.

Before you move on to the next thing on the list, take a moment to close your eyes. Don't reach for a book. Refuse to look at your phone. Keep your thoughts from wandering away. And simply fix your heart on the one who loves you. Think about His compassion. Dwell on His promises. Consider His majesty, and the army of angels He commands. Have faith in the one He sent so you can forever be with Him.

Whether you need comfort, encouragement, or protection, He is the answer. Look first in His direction for clarity and understanding. He is close at hand and forever unchanging.

LORD, THANK YOU FOR SHOWING ME THAT YOU ARE MY EVERYTHING. THROUGH EVERY DAY, THROUGH EVERY YEAR, I NEED ONLY TO FIX MY EYES ON YOU—THE AUTHOR AND PERFECTER OF MY FAITH.

Your Inmost Heart

Behold, You desire truth in the inner being;
make me therefore to know wisdom in my inmost heart.
Psalm 51:6 AMPC

Psalm 51 was written by David after his adultery with Bathsheba and the murder of her husband, Uriah. What had begun for David as a nice view of a woman bathing on a rooftop later ended in death, family tragedy, and his separation from God.

Sin is not just in your actions but begins in your heart, a place from which anyone can stray from the Way if she is not honest with herself and God.

Proverbs 4:23–27 gives some ideas of how to keep our hearts in check: "Keep vigilant watch over your heart; that's where life starts. Don't talk out of both sides of your mouth; avoid careless banter, white lies, and gossip. Keep your eyes straight ahead; ignore all sideshow distractions. Watch your step, and the road will stretch out smooth before you. Look neither right nor left; leave evil in the dust" (MSG).

When you are honest with yourself and God, true in your innermost heart of hearts, you will not stumble. But if or when you do mess up, go to God. Let Him know everything. . .even though He already knows. Ask His forgiveness and ask Him to make you a wiser woman.

LORD, HELP ME TO KEEP MY EYES ON YOU.
DEEP WITHIN, I LONG FOR YOUR TRUTH.
MAKE ME "HEART SMART" AS I WALK IN YOUR WAY.

By Grace

But whatever I am now, it is all because God poured out his special favor on me—and not without results. For I have worked harder than any of the other apostles; yet it was not I but God who was working through me by his grace.

1 Corinthians 15:10 NLT

He can make the sick well. He can make the blind see. He can bring the dead to life again. He can turn doubters into believers and murderers into miracle workers.

Yet, we sometimes fall into the habit of thinking that God cannot do anything with us—that the God who crafted Saul the persecutor into Paul the evangelist cannot change us and use us to expand His kingdom.

Even Paul felt he was "not even worthy to be called an apostle" (1 Corinthians 15:9 NLT). But the difference between Paul and many others who feel unworthy is that Paul didn't let his feelings get in the way of God's faithfulness. Grace does that for us. Grace gives us a position we have no right to take and access to power we have no authority to use, in exchange for nothing we can do or deserve.

Grace is the beautiful, life-changing, heart-shaping gift of your loving God. Whatever you are or will be is because of His grace.

LORD, THANK YOU FOR YOUR GIFT OF GRACE.
HELP ME TO USE IT TO WORK FOR YOU. AMEN.

Praise and Worship

It is good to give thanks to the Lord*, to sing praises to the Most High. It is good to proclaim your unfailing love in the morning, your faithfulness in the evening. . . . I sing for joy because of what you have done.*

Psalm 92:1–2, 4 NLT

A melody preps the audience for a poignant scene in a movie. A band blasts a rousing tune to pump up the crowd at a stadium. Music has the ability to move us. If we choose to, praising God will set the tone for our lives.

God is worthy of worship. Our praises rise to Him and please His heart. *Our* hearts are affected by praise too, especially in our difficulties. Note the psalmist's words of praise that sandwich troubling reality: "O Lord, what great works you do! . . . The wicked sprout like weeds and evildoers flourish. . . . But you, O Lord, will be exalted forever" (Psalm 92:5, 7–8 NLT). Praise reminds us of truth. Our God is greatest even when evil seems to be greater. The wicked may riot now, but God will repay—He reigns forever.

It's good to sing praises to God. It's good at morning and evening. It's good *any*time. Out loud or in your heart, sing of God's faithfulness. Sing of His love. Sing of how great He is!

GOD, EVIL MAY CLAMOR, BUT YOU WILL HEAR MY PRAISE. GREAT ARE YOU!

Burden Bearing

*"For I give plenty of water to the weary ones,
and refresh everyone who languishes."*
JEREMIAH 31:25 NASB

What kind of burdens are you carrying today? Finances, health, work, family cares, children—they're all burdens we take on, thinking we have to work out all the problems and find the solutions.

Jesus tells us, "If you are tired from carrying heavy burdens, come to me and I will give you rest. Take the yoke I give you. Put it on your shoulders and learn from me. I am gentle and humble, and you will find rest. This yoke is easy to bear, and this burden is light" (Matthew 11:28–30 CEV). While these verses primarily refer to the burdens of guilt and shame over sin and our inability to release those burdens on our own, a secondary meaning applies to the burdens we take on ourselves by not trusting God's sovereignty in every area of our lives.

Several times in scripture, we humans are compared to sheep. Sheep are not burden-bearing animals. You don't see shepherds loading them up like mules, camels, and horses. Neither are we required to take on burdens. The fact is that many times in God's Word we're encouraged to roll every burden onto *Him*.

The promised result is God's rest—His peace, His refreshing of our spirits—in spite of any problems we face. When we submit to His yoke, we find that the burden truly is light and easy to bear. No longer languishing, we find ourselves refreshed, walking forward in His strength.

FATHER GOD, MAY I HEED JESUS' INVITATION TODAY, KNOWING THAT YOUR DESIRE IS TO DO ALL THINGS FOR MY GOOD AND YOUR GLORY.

Dust

Just as a father has compassion on his children, so the LORD has compassion on those who fear Him. For He Himself knows our form; He is mindful that we are nothing but dust.

PSALM 103:13–14 NASB

Do you ever feel weak or inconsequential? Or like the slightest wind of difficulty could just blow you away? These verses tell you that you are but dust and that God is aware of that. That doesn't sound very encouraging, does it? But when you think about it, great strength can be gleaned from this truth.

The Lord knows your frame. He knows that at times you are prone to weakness and worry and lack the strength to continue. So if you are harboring guilt that you have not lived up to some heavenly standard that you feel God has placed on you, release that guilt. He is mindful of what you are capable of and doesn't ask that you be some kind of superwoman. This is not an excuse for complacency or laziness, but an encouragement that your efforts are recognized and smiled on by God.

Even though you are but a speck of dust in the history of the universe, God has compassion on you and knows you as a father knows his child. How stunning! It doesn't matter that you sometimes feel weak and inconsequential—the Most High God knows and loves you. In that truth resides all the strength and value you need.

LORD, THANK YOU THAT YOU KNOW MY FRAME. PLEASE GRANT ME THE STRENGTH AND VALUE THAT I LONG FOR.

Jesus' Plea

"Jerusalem, Jerusalem, you who kill the prophets and stone those sent to you, how often I have longed to gather your children together, as a hen gathers her chicks under her wings, and you were not willing."

LUKE 13:34 NIV

You can feel the anguish in His words. It's the kind of pain in a mother's cries for her child who has run away—again. It's the loving anger you see in a father's pressed-together lips when his child has been led astray by some predatory friends. It's the weary grief of the guardian who feels like she's talking to a brick wall instead of an adolescent.

Anyone who has been a parent or caregiver will recognize this plea. "I just want you to be safe," Jesus seems to say. "I want to take care of you if you will only let Me."

So many times you turn Jesus away without even realizing it. You choose to ignore your own sin issues, weave webs of deceit that even fool yourself, and turn to other comforts that only seek to destroy you. Jesus calls out to you then: "Daughter, you who run away from the only one who can save you, I just want to love you. Please turn and let Me give you forgiveness and peace."

Open your ears to this heart cry of Jesus. If you have been running, turn around. Let Him love you. If you haven't, just rest in Him today.

LORD, LET ME STAY UNDER YOUR WING. AMEN.

What Are You Waiting For?

"Woe to you, Chorazin! Woe to you, Bethsaida! For if the mighty works done in you had been done in Tyre and Sidon, they would have repented long ago."
LUKE 10:13 ESV

When God brings a sin to your attention, how do you respond? Do you hem and haw a bit before admitting the wrong and asking for forgiveness? Do you drag your feet before making changes?

Dealing with sin in our lives isn't easy, but as God transforms us from the inside to be more like Christ, repenting of bad behavior and living in obedience is vital. We shouldn't close our ears to the things God calls us to do and be like the unrepentant cities that Jesus spoke about. And why would we not *want* to repent? Think on what Moses told Israel: "All these blessings shall come upon you and overtake you, if you obey the voice of the LORD your God. Blessed shall you be in the city, and blessed shall you be in the field. . . . Blessed shall you be when you come in, and blessed shall you be when you go out" (Deuteronomy 28:2–3, 6 ESV). Our loving heavenly Father reaches out to us with blessing in place of woe. He offers forgiveness if only we'll repent.

Is God whispering to your heart? Don't wait.

FATHER, YOU'VE BEEN REVEALING A SIN IN MY LIFE, AND I'VE BEEN IGNORING IT. PLEASE FORGIVE ME AND HELP ME START FRESH.

Good News!

"But for you who fear my name, the Sun of Righteousness will rise with healing in his wings. And you will go free, leaping with joy like calves let out to pasture. On the day when I act, you will tread upon the wicked as if they were dust under your feet."

MALACHI 4:2–3 NLT

If it seems like you're constantly bombarded with bad news. . .if you ever find yourself in a difficult place. . .if your faith is faltering and your heart is hopeless. . .if you feel alone and abandoned. . .there's good news for you, dear one!

If you're a faithful follower of Jesus, you're on the receiving end of bountiful blessings. And they're yours for the taking. Part of those blessings includes ultimate healing, joy, and freedom in Christ. How can you know this for certain? Because the promises of God's Word are unfaltering and trustworthy. If His Word says it, you can believe it! "GOD always does what he says, and is gracious in everything he does" (Psalm 145:13 MSG).

Today, thank God for making you one of His own. Praise Him for His saving grace. He is the one and only Redeemer!

FATHER GOD, BECAUSE OF YOUR STEADFAST LOVE AND GRACE, I AM FREE. I HAVE JOY IN MY HEART—EVEN WHEN LIFE IS HARD. YOU GIVE ME HOPE, NOT JUST FOR TODAY BUT FOR THE FUTURE. I CHOOSE TO FOLLOW YOU ALL THE DAYS OF MY LIFE. THANK YOU! AMEN.

Choose Life

"The thief comes only to steal and kill and destroy;
I have come that they may have life, and have it to the full."
JOHN 10:10 NIV

Too often, it seems as if the negatives of life outweigh the positives. The bills are piling up and it's a juggling act to see who gets paid this month. Your loved one needs to have special care during the upcoming treatments. You're exhausted and lacking mental focus. Life begins to cave in around you. It's just too much!

God's Word, though, shows us the lie—and the liar—behind those defeating thoughts. We have an enemy who delights in our believing such negative things, an enemy who wants only destruction for our souls. But Jesus came to give us life! We only have to choose it, as an act of the will blended with faith.

God is always a gentleman—He's not going to force His life on us. But when we rely on Him alone, He'll enable us to not only survive but *thrive* in our daily routines.

Each day, let's make a conscious decision to take hold of what Christ offers us—life, to the full.

LOVING LORD, HELP ME DAILY TO CHOOSE YOU AND THE LIFE YOU WANT TO GIVE ME. GIVE ME THE EYES OF FAITH TO TRUST THAT YOU WILL ENABLE ME TO SERVE LOVINGLY.

Get Up and Try Again

But may the God of all grace, who called us to His eternal glory by Christ Jesus, after you have suffered a while, perfect, establish, strengthen, and settle you.

1 PETER 5:10 NKJV

Have you ever fallen down in your Christian walk? It doesn't mean you are no longer a Christian, but you stumbled over something in your path that caused you to lose your footing. Perhaps you didn't see the obstacle in time. It's painful to fall, and sometimes it's hard to get up and continue on. While you're lying on the ground spiritually, Satan uses this opportunity to taunt you and accuse you. "You're not really a Christian. If you were, you wouldn't have fallen. You wouldn't have made a mistake. God doesn't need people like you. He's tired of fooling with you. Why don't you just give up?"

Sound familiar? Not only does it sound familiar, but if you're not careful, you will begin to believe it. The shame and remorse you feel because of your shortcoming only add to the lie Satan has just whispered in your ear. Don't listen to any more of his lies. God is a God of grace. The key is to stand up from the place where you have fallen and allow God to restore you, strengthen you, and establish you. He is faithful to His people.

LORD, FORGIVE MY SHORTCOMINGS AND EXTEND GRACE ONCE MORE TO YOUR SERVANT. GIVE ME STRENGTH TO CONTINUE THE RACE.

This Is the Way

The heart of the wise inclines to the right,
but the heart of the fool to the left.
ECCLESIASTES 10:2 NIV

Perhaps you are tired of all the confusion life presents. Somehow you may have lost your way, veered off the path. Distractions, selfishness, grief, and disappointment have pushed you in the wrong direction for too long. You lie in bed wide awake, unable to sleep, thoughts spinning around and around.

You turn off the droning television, walk to the nearest prayer nook, and search for your Bible. Wait. It may have been a very long time since you last opened it. Perhaps the best place to start is with prayer.

You sit and have a chat with the one who has loved you since the beginning of time and longs to hear your voice. Tears flow. You begin to pray: *God, I'm lost. I'm confused. I'm sorry I stepped away from You. I need You. Please forgive me. Show me what to do.*

Suddenly you feel snug and warm in the once chilly house. You feel God's familiar embrace and hear a soft whisper: "I've always been with you." Your eyes open. Then you spy your Bible and, with a smile, pull it out from underneath a stack of books and begin reading.

GOD, THANK YOU FOR STICKING WITH ME ALL THE WAY. HELP ME KEEP MY FEET ON YOUR PATH.

Flourish

But the godly will flourish like palm trees and grow strong like the cedars of Lebanon.
PSALM 92:12 NLT

God never intended for us to live subpar lives. He desires His very best for us. Sure, we'll walk through valleys. We'll trudge through hard times. But even during those seasons, He longs for us to flourish, like leaves on a healthy vine. For when we're tied into Him, when we've given heart, mind, soul, and thoughts to Him, we receive the nourishment we need to overcome and to experience victories that make no sense in the natural world.

So how do you begin the process of flourishing? Picture yourself like a small rosebush, freshly planted. Allow your roots to sink down deep in His Word. Let the water of His Spirit saturate the deepest places, removing any pain or unforgiveness. Then allow the sunlight of His presence to strengthen you from the inside out. Before long you'll be strong and hearty, a woman transformed.

FATHER, I WANT TO FLOURISH. I DON'T WANT TO LIVE A SUBPAR LIFE, ONE WHERE I'M JUST BARELY SCRAPING BY. I WANT THE FULLNESS THAT COMES WITH KNOWING AND LOVING YOU. HOLD ME CLOSE, I PRAY, THAT I MIGHT RECEIVE ALL YOU HAVE FOR ME. FEED, WATER, NOURISH. . .THAT I MIGHT FLOURISH AND GROW STRONG IN YOU. AMEN.

It's Taken Care Of

Everyone has to die once, then face the consequences.
Christ's death was also a one-time event,
but it was a sacrifice that took care of sins forever.
HEBREWS 9:27–28 MSG

How many sins have you committed today? Three? Five? Ten? How many sins did you commit yesterday? About the same? What about the day before? How many are you planning to commit tomorrow?

If you're like most, you've committed some doozies, probably more than you could ever add up. And if you ever *did* tally them, you would be mortified at the sheer number of times you've broken the heart of God—either with your actions or your thoughts and motivations.

Take another look at today's verse. What do you think it means when it says that Christ's death was a "one-time event" but "took care of sins forever"? Is it possible that something Jesus did two thousand years ago could take care of your transgressions today. . .and tomorrow? The answer is a resounding yes!

No matter what you've done, no matter where you've been, Jesus' sacrifice on the cross was powerful enough to wash away your sins. There's one thing you have to do, though. . .ask. Ask Him into your heart. Ask for His forgiveness. Then accept His free gift of salvation and breathe a huge sigh of relief as forgiveness flows freely.

LORD, I'M SO GRATEFUL YOU'VE TAKEN CARE OF MY SIN. IT'S WASHED IN THE BLOOD OF JESUS, NEVER TO BE SEEN AGAIN. THANK YOU, LORD! AMEN.

Beans or Steak?

Each of you must bring a gift in proportion to the way the LORD your God has blessed you.
DEUTERONOMY 16:17 NIV

At the harvest celebration, every Jew was to thank God with a sacrifice according to the blessings he'd been given. God's Word assumes that every believer would receive a blessing of some sort. At the very least, His people were alive because He provided food for them. Those who didn't have much more than that would bring a small but heartfelt offering. Others, blessed with physical abundance, brought a generous offering of much greater material value.

Our blessings may not be the kind we'd like: We may, for example, look for extra money to pay off bills while God sends us spiritual strength. But just as God provided for His Old Testament people even in the years of lean harvests, He provides for us.

We may be eating more beans and rice than steak and lobster, but isn't the former better for us in the long run? While we're looking for the good life, God's looking at what's good for us. Sometimes that means physical blessing—but other times it's a spiritual challenge.

No matter what our circumstances, God is blessing us—if we're following Him with steadfastness. Let's bless Him in return with our thanksgiving.

LORD, I THANK YOU FOR THE MANY BLESSINGS YOU GIVE. IN EXCHANGE, I OFFER YOU THE GIFT OF MY HEART AND LIFE.

Unfailing Love Surrounds Us

Many sorrows come to the wicked, but unfailing love surrounds those who trust the Lord.

Psalm 32:10 NLT

When you read this verse, what is the first thing that comes to mind? Maybe that evil people will face many sorrows, but you will be surrounded by the Lord's unfailing love. You will be surrounded with love because you are a good person, and far from evil! Right?

But what if this verse is saying something else? As we read through the Bible, we see that we are all wicked. "No one is righteous—not even one" (Romans 3:10 NLT). No one is good. That is, except through the grace of God. Maybe, then, this verse is saying that many sorrows will come to the wicked—to humankind—but those who choose to put their trust in the Lord, in Christ Jesus, will be surrounded by His unfailing love. Those people may face trouble because they are still in a world full of fallen people, but they will not face it alone.

No matter what you may be facing, let this be your anthem. Let this be the promise you hold close to your heart. Let it be a verse you recite to yourself as you fall asleep at night. "Many sorrows come to the wicked, but unfailing love surrounds those who trust the Lord."

I HAVE THIS PROMISE TO HOLD ON TO. LORD, REMEMBER ME. REMEMBER HOW I PUT MY TRUST IN YOU AND SEEK YOU DAY AND NIGHT. SURROUND ME WITH YOUR UNFAILING LOVE, THAT I MAY WALK THROUGH THIS LIFE KNOWING THAT I AM SECURE IN YOUR HANDS.

Fullness

I pray that you, being rooted and established in love, may have power. . .to know this love that surpasses knowledge—that you may be filled to the measure of all the fullness of God.

Ephesians 3:17–19 niv

God's fullness infuses you when you understand how deeply you are *loved,* to the brim.

What keeps you from accepting God's love? Perhaps feelings of unworthiness and guilt block your heart. Or the shame of secret sins isolates you. Yet the one who knows you best accepts you completely. Christ's blood was more than sufficient, and you stand before God faultless and beloved. Let go of any thought that you must *earn* the affection that God pours into you freely.

The fullness of God is like the deep pool at the base of a mountain waterfall, deep enough for you to plunge into, laughing with joy. Immerse yourself in the great, incomprehensible mystery of who God is—an all-knowing and all-powerful being who *chooses* friendship with you. He is enduringly faithful but forgives all your unfaithfulness. He is God, the mighty warrior of the Old Testament—and He is Christ, the gentle Lamb of the New.

Though God is unfathomable, He delights in revealing Himself to you so that you may be filled to the brim with the fullness of God.

FATHER GOD, HELP ME ABSORB THE DEEP AND EXTRAVAGANT LOVE WITH WHICH YOU FILL ME TO THE BRIM. AMEN.

God Delights in Repentance

"Those whom I love, I reprove and discipline, so be zealous and repent. Behold, I stand at the door and knock. If anyone hears my voice and opens the door, I will come in to him and eat with him, and he with me."

Revelation 3:19–20 ESV

The Laodicean church is famous for being "lukewarm"—neither on fire for God nor totally cold. But what follows its rebuke is today's verse: God's promise that those He loves, He disciplines—He provides opportunity for repentance so that fellowship with Him can be restored.

Amos contains the same promise. Israel had committed "mighty sins": She afflicted the just, took bribes, and sent the needy away (Amos 5:12 NKJV). Tired of her empty religious festivals, God wanted to see "justice roll down like waters, and righteousness like an ever-flowing stream" (Amos 5:24 ESV). But despite her sins and the discipline He'd already sent, God would heal Israel if she turned back to Him.

It's the same with us: We cannot go so far away from God that He will not hear our cries for forgiveness, our sincere return to Him and His ways. God keeps seeking us—knocking at the door of our hearts—and if we respond to His call, He will fellowship with us anew.

JESUS, ARE YOU KNOCKING ON MY HEART TODAY? WHAT DOORS HAVE I KEPT SHUT FROM YOU? ENCOURAGE ME TO OPEN THEM AND TURN BACK TO YOU.

The Shortest Psalm

O praise the Lord, all you nations! Praise Him, all you people! For His mercy and loving-kindness are great toward us, and the truth and faithfulness of the Lord endure forever. Praise the Lord! (Hallelujah!)

Psalm 117:1–2 AMPC

Psalm 117 (containing only two verses) is the shortest psalm and the shortest chapter in the Bible. But it's so full of wonderful truths that can spark more than a million and one words of praise. It first tells God's people to worship Him, the whole world to sing praises. Then it explains why: because the Lord's mercy and love for you is never-ending and unchangeable. God wants you to know this and believe it!

Isn't the idea of a stable and strong heavenly Father so comforting to hear when this life feels anything but normal? God doesn't have mood swings or change His mind. His love for His daughters doesn't shift because of what they do. It is entirely based on who He is.

This is a comfort that will hopefully push you to seek Him and His will. God wants to say to every one of His daughters today, "Loving you is so easy." Embrace this goodness and praise Him for His everlasting care.

LORD, I'M SO THANKFUL FOR YOUR MERCY AND LOVE FOR ME. I DON'T THINK I'LL EVER BE ABLE TO DEFINE FULLY WHAT IT MEANS FOR YOU TO ALWAYS BE THERE FOR ME. BUT I PRAISE YOU, MY ROCK AND REFUGE, ALL THE SAME!

Comfort Food

For whatever things were written before were written for our learning, that we through the patience and comfort of the Scriptures might have hope.

ROMANS 15:4 NKJV

A big mound of ice cream topped with hot fudge; a full bowl of salty, buttery popcorn; grilled cheese sandwiches and warm chicken noodle soup fixed by Mom—comfort food. There is nothing like a generous helping of things that bring the sensation of comfort to a worn body at the end of a long day or to a bruised mind after a disappointment. Those comfort foods soothe the body and mind because, through the senses, they remind us of happier and more secure times.

Romans 15:4 tells us that the scriptures are comfort food for the soul. They were written and given so that, through our learning, we would be comforted with the truths of God. Worldly pleasures bring a temporary comfort, but the problem still remains when the pleasure or comfort fades. However, the words of God are soothing and provide permanent hope and peace. Through God's Word, you will be changed, and your troubles will dim in the bright light of Christ. So the next time you are sad, lonely, or disappointed, before you turn to pizza, turn to the Word of God as your source of comfort.

THANK YOU, FATHER, FOR THE RICH COMFORT YOUR WORD PROVIDES. HELP ME TO REMEMBER TO FIND MY COMFORT IN SCRIPTURE RATHER THAN THROUGH EARTHLY THINGS THAT WILL ULTIMATELY FAIL ME. AMEN.

He Knows You

How precious are your thoughts about me, O God. They cannot be numbered! I can't even count them; they outnumber the grains of sand! And when I wake up, you are still with me!

PSALM 139:17–18 NLT

Did you know that you have a history with God? Your relationship is ever growing, ever changing, and He knows you. He knit you together in your mother's womb. He's watched as you've grown up. He's seen every good day. Every bad day. Not a moment passes that He's unaware of what you're up to.

And He still loves you. When you live in relationship with Him, covered by the sacrifice of Christ, He doesn't see the things you've done wrong. Don't walk into this day feeling the weight of your failures and imagining there is no way He could continue to love you. He does love you, even through the worst of times. Sending His Son while we were still sinners is proof of that love (see Romans 5:8).

So instead of coming before Him full of shame and with a heavy heart, come before Him in humble thankfulness and confidence that He loves you so much. When you come before Him, He is pleased to see His daughter—spotless and whole. He is willing—and desires—to have a deep and thriving relationship with you.

LORD, I CAN NEVER FULLY UNDERSTAND THE GRACE WITH WHICH YOU LOVE ME. I AM FOREVER AMAZED AND FILLED WITH JOY. LET OUR RELATIONSHIP GROW DEEPER THROUGH THIS DAY AND THE DAYS AHEAD.

Joy to Your Soul!

The Lord is good, a refuge in times of trouble.
He cares for those who trust in him.
Nahum 1:7 NIV

Indeed, the Lord is good and slow to anger, and He is your refuge.

But when you read on about the city of Nineveh in the book of Nahum, you will see that the Lord's patience doesn't last forever when people are bent on living a wicked life. Many parallels to today's world can be seen in these warnings to Nineveh. The sins once considered wrong in society just a few decades ago are now considered acceptable behavior, perhaps even celebrated. Good is now called evil, and evil good.

So how can you live to please the Almighty when all the fallen earth seems once again determined to disobey God's laws? Pray with a humble heart. Listen to the Lord and His still, small voice. Read His Word. Stay in fellowship with Christians who believe the Bible is truly the holy Word of God, not just a book of general guidelines. Come before God with a willingness to say, "I've wronged you, Lord. I'm sorry." And mean it.

The good news is that when you do repent, the Lord is gracious to forgive and put you back in intimate fellowship with Him. Repentance isn't a burden. It will lighten your load and bring joy to your soul!

JESUS, GIVE ME A MEEK HEART. SHOW ME MY SINS, THEN GIVE ME THE COURAGE TO CONFESS THEM AND RECEIVE THE PEACE OF YOUR FORGIVENESS. AMEN.

Marvelous

But even before I was born, God chose me
and called me by his marvelous grace.
Galatians 1:15 NLT

What is so astonishing about the grace of God? What is it that makes us read about it and think about it in absolute wonder? Its very existence is a miracle. To be given this position of favor and blessing—this gift of forgiveness and restoration—without even asking for it or having done some act of penitence or completed some method of atonement ourselves, is more than we can even comprehend.

Certainly, giving to others is an action we can see as good and helpful. But even that act of kindness is something we do because it feels good or because we feel we have a duty to do it. But God does not need us to make Him feel good. And He has no obligation to us—He doesn't owe us anything.

No, in fact God had made His plans and included us in them long before we ever even took a breath. Before our tiny fingers were able to hold a Bible, God had constructed the story of His people. And before we were able to squeak out the notes about His amazing grace, God had already composed the sweet music of forgiveness.

LORD, I MARVEL AT YOUR NEVER-
ENDING KINDNESS AND LOVE. AMEN.

Impossibly Blessed

"Blessed is she who has believed that the Lord would fulfill his promises to her!"
LUKE 1:45 NIV

It's one thing to be told something amazing is coming your way. It's quite another thing to actually believe it.

In Luke 1:26–32, God sent the angel Gabriel to Mary, telling her she had been chosen to give birth to a son. He said, "Do not be afraid, Mary; you have found favor with God. You will conceive and give birth to a son, and you are to call him Jesus. He will be great and will be called the Son of the Most High" (verses 30-32 NIV).

When Mary asked how this would happen, Gabriel explained the Holy Spirit would come upon her and the power of the Most High God would overshadow her. To this, Mary simply said, "I am the Lord's servant. . . . May your word to me be fulfilled" (Luke 1:38 NIV). In other words, Mary believed God's promise. And it was that belief that became a joyous blessing.

Woman of the Way, remember that God will *always* fulfill His promises! Take comfort and ease in that knowledge. Then, like Mary, you too can rejoice! You too are blessed by God's promises! No shaking, no doubt, no fear can enter that equation.

DEAR GOD, PLEASE BLESS ME, AS YOU BLESSED MARY. HELP ME TO HAVE FAITH, TO ASK THAT YOUR WORD BE FULFILLED. HELP ME TO BELIEVE SO THAT I MAY BE IMPOSSIBLY BLESSED.

Your Heart's Desire

Trust in the L*ORD and do good. Then you will live safely in the land and prosper. Take delight in the* L*ORD, and he will give you your heart's desires. Commit everything you do to the* L*ORD. Trust him, and he will help you.*

PSALM 37:3–5 NLT

It's easy to look at this passage and think, *Hey, if I just delight in the Lord, He'll give me everything I want!* But when we really start to delight in the Lord, God changes our hearts so completely that all we ever want is what *He* wants. When you commit everything you do to the Lord, you will begin to see how your desires line up with God's desires.

What does this look like in everyday life? Start your morning with thankfulness. Ask God to bless your day and to provide opportunities to be a blessing to those you encounter. Interact with God about each issue and problem you face. Thank Him for big and little blessings that come your way. Seek His will and guidance when you make plans. Pray for loved ones that don't know Christ. Intercede for friends and neighbors who need divine help. Be on the lookout for new ways to delight yourself in the Lord.

LORD, I COMMIT MY WHOLE HEART TO YOU—AND ALL OF MY PLANS AND IDEAS. I WANT YOUR WILL IN MY LIFE. THANK YOU FOR YOUR BLESSINGS AND YOUR GREAT LOVE FOR ME. SHOW ME HOW TO DELIGHT IN YOU, LORD. I LOVE YOU. AMEN.

Rescued

"Sirs, what must I do to be saved?" So they said, "Believe on the Lord Jesus Christ, and you will be saved."
ACTS 16:30–31 NKJV

Many people think that we have to qualify for heaven, that gaining eternal life is like being in a deep ditch with slippery sides. We scramble up as much as we can. God reaches down and does the rest.

This misconception has two problems. First, God does not need our help! Jesus paid the penalty for our sins when He died in our place and said, "It is finished," meaning: "Paid in full!" Second, the Bible says that eternal life is a free gift. We can do nothing to earn it, deserve it, or pay God back. We receive it by faith, not by works. "For by grace you have been saved through faith, and that not of yourselves; it is the gift of God, not of works" (Ephesians 2:8–9 NKJV).

A better analogy for eternal life pictures us drowning in sin. We cannot save ourselves. The nail-pierced hand of Jesus reaches out to us. If our response is, "Lord, save me!" He does. "Whoever believes in Him [will] not perish but have everlasting life" (John 3:16 NKJV).

Where are you spiritually? Still in the slippery ditch, trying in vain to claw your way up to God? Or have you trusted in Christ alone to rescue you from sin and save you forever?

LORD JESUS, I AM A SINNER WHO DESERVES THE PUNISHMENT OF SPIRITUAL DEATH. THANK YOU FOR DYING IN MY PLACE AND GUARANTEEING ME ETERNAL LIFE BECAUSE I HAVE PUT MY FAITH IN YOU AND NOTHING ELSE.

On the Run—with God

O God, You are my God, earnestly will I seek You; my inner self thirsts for You, my flesh longs and is faint for You, in a dry and weary land where no water is.

PSALM 63:1 AMPC

Absalom, King David's son, was attempting to overthrow his father. So David fled his palace, his comforts, his people. Cursed, then pelted with stones and dirt (see 2 Samuel 16), this weary and beleaguered king wrote Psalm 63 in the wilderness of Judah.

There David remembered God's power and glory. He recalled His loving-kindness, knowing that it is more precious than life itself. And in spite of all that was happening in his life, David told God, "So will I bless You while I live; I will lift up my hands in Your name" (verse 4 AMPC).

Even though David was on the run once again, even though he was out of his comfort zone, he hadn't forgotten the most important things: his love, worship, and pursuit of God.

When all seems lost in your life, when those who once loved you now curse you, when you are relegated to a barren wasteland, remember Psalm 63. Know that the most important thing you have—faith in God—is there for you to cling to and rejoice in. He is all the comfort you need, no matter where you are.

YOU, LORD, ARE MY ALL IN ALL. YOU ALONE ARE MY COMFORT ZONE. YOU ARE ALL I NEED.

Nothing but Good Plans

In times of trouble, may the Lord *answer your cry. May the name of the God of Jacob keep you safe from all harm. May he send you help from his sanctuary and strengthen you from Jerusalem. May he remember all your gifts and look favorably on your burnt offerings. . . . May he grant your heart's desires and make all your plans succeed. May we shout for joy when we hear of your victory and raise a victory banner in the name of our God. May the* Lord *answer all your prayers.*

Psalm 20:1–5 NLT

Do you believe 100 percent, without a doubt, that the heavenly Father will answer *all* your prayers? Not that He will say yes to your every request—but that He will answer with a yes, no, or maybe later?

Whether you're asking God for hope, healing, help, or safety from harm, you can know with certainty that He will do what's best for you—He has nothing but good plans for you, sister! His promise in Jeremiah 29:11 (NIV) says, "For I know the plans I have for you. . .plans to prosper you and not to harm you, plans to give you hope and a future."

So pray with complete confidence to the one who offers protection, strength, hope, and success and know that an answer is coming your way!

HEAVENLY FATHER, YOU LOVE ME AND WANT ONLY THE BEST FOR ME. THANK YOU FOR YOUR ANSWERS TO MY PRAYERS!

Lord, Please Be Gentle

I know, LORD, that our lives are not our own. We are not able to plan our own course. So correct me, LORD, but please be gentle.

JEREMIAH 10:23–24 NLT

We map out our route by filling up planners and calendars. We place firm but gentle grips at ten and two o'clock on the steering wheels of our lives. We merge lanes as we set goals and take the steps necessary to accomplish them. And then a humongous deer of a crisis bounds out of the woods onto our path and we realize—in one terrifying moment—that we don't have the control over our lives like we thought we did.

God's expert ability to plan our lives is so much better than ours, but it's often terrifying to give up that control. Jesus, in the garden of Gethsemane just hours before His arrest, trial, and crucifixion, admitted His own desire to alter God's plans when He prayed, "If it is possible, let this cup of suffering be taken away from me." But even in His struggle, He knew God's way was ultimately the best, most perfect way when He earnestly prayed, "Yet I want your will to be done, not mine" (Matthew 26:39 NLT).

"Your will, not mine" is a powerful and often scary prayer to pray. Just remember God's great love for you. Don't be afraid to ask and accept His gentle correction to your course.

FATHER, TAKE CONTROL.
BUT PLEASE BE GENTLE. AMEN.

At All Times

Pray in the Spirit at all times with all kinds of prayers.
EPHESIANS 6:18 NCV

When giving instructions about important things, it's good to be specific. The more specific the instructions, the more likely the task will be done correctly. That's why when Paul spoke to the Ephesians about praying, he didn't leave any question about when to pray.

Prayer isn't a ritual to practice before bed or first thing in the morning or when the sun is at a certain place in the sky. Though it's great to have specific times of concentrated, focused prayer, our conversations with God shouldn't be limited to a certain time on our calendars. God wants us to pray *all the time*.

After all, God wants to be included in our days. He wants to walk and talk with us each moment. Imagine if we traveled through the day with our children or our husbands, but we only spoke to them between 6:15 and 6:45 a.m.! Of course we'd never do that to the people we care about. God doesn't want us to do that to Him either.

God wants to travel the journey with us. He's a wonderful companion, offering wisdom and comfort for every aspect of our lives. But He can only do that if we let Him into our schedules, every minute of every day.

DEAR FATHER, THANK YOU FOR ALWAYS BEING THERE TO LISTEN. REMIND ME TO TALK TO YOU ABOUT EVERYTHING, ALL THE TIME. AMEN.

Let Your Thankfulness Show

In everything give thanks; for this is the will of God for you in Christ Jesus.

1 THESSALONIANS 5:18 NASB

You were probably taught from a young age to say "Thank you" when someone does something for you. Being thankful doesn't seem like a big deal. But in this verse, Paul asserts that being thankful is God's will for you. All of a sudden, thankfulness sounds like an essential part of our walk with God.

Those who are in Christ have abundant reason to be thankful. You were owned by and enslaved to the horrible master of sin. You were bought from him with a price that could never be repaid—the blood of a flawless Lamb. And not only were you rescued from a life of separation from God, but you were adopted into His family. You have been lavished with grace and love. The Lord has provided for you, brought you into a relationship with Him, and promised you an eternity with Him. He did all this, not because you could do something for Him, but just because He decided to place His love on you. It makes perfect sense that Paul would say your life should be characterized by thankfulness.

In a world where people exhibit an increasing sense of entitlement and self-centeredness, think of how much a thankful spirit will stand out to those around you. Everyone *is* entitled—to death and an eternity away from God. Be thankful, for God's will for you is infinitely better than anything you could deserve.

LORD, MAY I GRASP MORE FULLY WHAT YOU HAVE DONE FOR ME SO THAT MY LIFE BECOMES CHARACTERIZED BY THANKFULNESS.

The One You Can Count On

Blessed be the LORD my Rock, who trains my hands for war, and my fingers for battle—my lovingkindness and my fortress, my high tower and my deliverer, my shield and the One in whom I take refuge, who subdues my people under me.

PSALM 144:1–2 NKJV

David learned at an early age that he could count on God. Although small in stature, he killed a lion and a bear, protecting his father's sheep from certain death. His courage and boldness came from within, from strength in his relationship with God.

His brothers, onlookers, and especially his enemy, the Philistine giant Goliath, laughed at him when he stood before them declaring he would take down Israel's enemy. But David had faith that God would go before him and give him victory in the battles he faced.

God has been with you and prepared you for what lies before you. You don't have to go into battle alone. When you know God as the one you can always count on, you can stand in the face of the giants in your life and come out of your battle a giant slayer!

GOD, YOU ARE SO FAITHFUL. THANK YOU FOR BEING WITH ME IN THE BATTLES I'VE FACED. I KNOW I CAN COUNT ON YOU TO GO WITH ME NOW AND SEE ME THROUGH TO BECOME THE CHAMPION YOU HAVE DESTINED ME TO BE.

Everything Will Be Fine

"Get going. . . . I will send an angel before you. . . . I will personally go with you."
EXODUS 33:1–2, 14 NLT

God wanted Moses to lead His people to a new place, a land flowing with milk and honey. Yet that new place was one the Egyptian-born Moses had never seen! And he was not to just go there himself but to lead God's people there!

Moses knew he was special to God, so he earnestly prayed, "If it is true that you look favorably on me, let me know your ways so I may understand you more fully and continue to enjoy your favor" (Exodus 33:13 NLT). God replied, "I will personally go with you, Moses, and I will give you rest—everything will be fine for you" (Exodus 33:14 NLT).

When God calls you down a new path, know He'll be with you. Instead of focusing on the what-ifs and stressing about the details, trust God's plan for you.

Remember that because God favors you, His angel has already arrived in the place you're bound. So relax. God promises, "Everything will be fine for you" because you walk with Him. And God keeps His promises, just as He "keeps" you.

I'M NOT VERY FOND OF CHANGE, LORD. BUT I KNOW YOU WANT ME TO HEAD DOWN A DIFFERENT ROAD. SO LORD, HELP ME UNDERSTAND YOU MORE SO I CAN REST EASY AS WE WALK TOGETHER.

God of All the Earth

Shout for joy to God, all the earth; sing the glory of his name; give to him glorious praise! Say to God, "How awesome are your deeds! So great is your power that your enemies come cringing to you. All the earth worships you and sings praises to you."

Psalm 66:1–4 ESV

Do you tend to reserve your songs of praise for Sunday morning? Or do you sing praises for God's goodness throughout the week too?

In the verses above, the psalmist is calling *everyone* to joyfully praise God—after all, God is the God over all the earth, not just the God of Israel. The psalmist then follows with instruction on *how* to praise God: "Say to God, 'How awesome are your deeds!'" Praise involves telling God how amazing He is. . .what wonderful things He has done in your life. Praise celebrates His awesome power.

If praise doesn't come easily or naturally because your mind runs amok with thoughts full of doubt and fear, ask God to remind you that He's in control and will protect and care for you always. When you invite Him to take complete control, your worries will be replaced with joy—and, as thoughts of thanksgiving and hope fill your mind, praise will spill from your heart and lips!

FATHER GOD, YOU ARE GOD OF ALL THE EARTH. AND I AM SO THANKFUL. I WILL PRAISE YOU EVERY DAY OF MY LIFE! AMEN.

Start Your Day with God

In the morning, LORD, you hear my voice; in the morning I lay my requests before you and wait expectantly.

PSALM 5:3 NIV

Mornings are hard for a lot of people—especially night owls who get more done in the evenings. And verses like this one can tend to make night owls feel like they aren't as spiritual as those who get up early to be with God.

The reality is that God wants to be the very center of your life. He doesn't want to be at the top of your priority list—just another box to check off each day. He wants your heart and attention morning, noon, and night. You won't get more points with God if you read ten Bible verses before your morning cup of coffee.

So how can you start your day with God even if you haven't gotten up hours earlier for devotions? As you wake up in the morning, thank the Lord for a new day. Ask Him to control your thoughts and attitude as you make the bed. Thank Him for providing for you as you toast your bagel. Ask that your self-image be based on your relationship with Christ as you get dressed and brush your teeth. Continue to pray as you drive to work or school. Spend time in His Word throughout the day. End your day by thanking Him for His love and faithfulness.

God wants a constant relationship with you, and He is available and waiting to do life with you twenty-four hours a day.

DEAR LORD, THANK YOU FOR THE GIFT OF A NEW DAY. HELP ME BE AWARE OF YOUR CONSTANT PRESENCE IN MY LIFE. AMEN.

The Right Tools for the Job

By his divine power, God has given us everything we need for living a godly life. We have received all of this by coming to know him, the one who called us to himself by means of his marvelous glory and excellence.

2 PETER 1:3 NLT

Have you ever tried to hang a picture without a hammer? Or make a dress without a sewing machine? Or bake a pie without an oven? Trying to do a job without the right tools can be difficult, inefficient, and even impossible. Having the right tools for the job can mean the difference between frustration and success.

As we journey through the Christian life, we may feel frustration. We may feel like we lack the patience to deal with a difficult husband, or the forgiveness to let go of anger toward someone who has hurt us. We may become tired and discouraged, lacking the energy to continue in the Lord's work. But the Bible promises us that God has already given us everything we need. From time to time, the tools we need may not seem readily available, but we can hold tight to the truth that His divine power has made them available to us. The more we come to know Him, the more we realize our calling. We can be assured that He will equip us with everything we need to do His work.

FATHER, THANK YOU FOR YOUR DIVINE POWER AND FOR GIVING ME EVERYTHING I NEED TO LIVE THE CHRISTIAN LIFE. WHEN I FEEL DISCOURAGED, REMIND ME TO SEEK TO KNOW YOU MORE SO THAT I CAN EXPERIENCE YOUR GREAT AND PERFECT PROMISES. AMEN.

Constant and Continual

Jesus, replying, said to them, Have faith in God [constantly].
MARK 11:22 AMPC

This faith thing isn't a once-and-done deal, nor is it something to be thrown away at the first sign of trouble or forgotten when all is well. It's a persistent, dogged, determined belief in God.

This faith is the constant belief that a beneficent force, one that sustains and propels everything around you—from the tiniest of ant colonies to the farthest of planets—is blessing, guarding, watching, and keeping you; smiling down, bursting to favor you with gifts galore; looking you in the face and giving "you peace (tranquility of heart and life *continually*)" (Numbers 6:26 AMPC, emphasis added).

Your only part is to be constant in your faith. And the only way to do that is to spend lots of time with God. When you do, His part is to continually give you peace—within and without—no matter what is going on in your life.

God has created you to be with Him, so abide in Him. He has given you His Son Jesus to guide you in all things, so follow Him. He has left behind His Spirit to comfort you, so cling to Him. This faith is fed and fueled by your actively spending time with the greatest of beings—Father, Son, and Spirit. Do your part (He is already doing His) and you will have a constant, living faith and a continual, abiding peace.

HERE I AM, GOD. LET'S TALK.

Changed by Love

He escorts me to the banquet hall;
it's obvious how much he loves me.
SONG OF SOLOMON 2:4 NLT

There are several interpretations of the imagery in the book we know as the Song of Solomon. But whatever you think about the symbolism and the characters being represented in these verses of poetry, one thing is certain. This is a song about love and how love affects the way we look at one another and at the world around us.

When we fall in love, a beautiful transformation takes place. A person, who perhaps a day before was just like anyone else walking on the streets, suddenly becomes beautiful to us—precious. Someone we want near us. Someone we want to know every little thing about. Someone we want to know us.

And that same beautiful transformation happens to everyone through the love of Christ—including you. Instead of nothing special, you become one of the favored ones of the King of kings. Instead of being lost in sin, you are found at His feet. Instead of being an embattled soul, you become an instrument of His peace. And instead of being a stranger on the street, you become a guest of honor at His banquet table.

It should be obvious to us how much God loves us—it is written all over His hands and feet.

LORD, THANK YOU FOR LOVING ME SO COMPLETELY. AMEN.

Gracious Spirit

Answer me quickly, LORD; my spirit fails. Don't hide Your face from me, or I will be like those going down to the Pit. Let me experience Your faithful love in the morning, for I trust in You. Reveal to me the way I should go because I long for You. Rescue me from my enemies, LORD; I come to You for protection. Teach me to do Your will, for You are my God. May Your gracious Spirit lead me on level ground.

PSALM 143:7–10 HCSB

David prayed to God for answers. He prayed for God's loving presence, help, protection, wisdom, and knowledge. He prayed for the grace of the Spirit to lead and guide him.

David's humble pleas revealed just how much he wanted his thoughts, heart, and actions to line up with God's and His call on his life.

Perhaps David's words resonate with you. Perhaps today you are looking to God for an answer, for more of His presence and wisdom, for the power of the Holy Spirit to move in your life and the lives of others, for the Lord's grace to abound, to lead you to level ground.

In this moment, take some time to quiet your mind, heart, and body through prayer. Let God's gracious Spirit touch you in a way that shows you just how precious you—a dearly loved daughter of the King—are.

GRACIOUS GOD, I COME TO YOU NOW.
I NEED YOUR WISDOM AND PRESENCE.

The Simple Things

In him our hearts rejoice, for we trust in his holy name.

Psalm 33:21 niv

Think about the simple pleasures in everyday life—that first sip of coffee in the morning, waking up to realize you still have a few more minutes to sleep, or putting on fresh, warm clothes right out of the dryer on a cold winter morning. Perhaps it's a walk along the beach or a hike up the mountains into the blue skies that gives you a simple peace.

God knows all the simple pleasures you enjoy—and He created them for your delight. When the simple things that can come only by His hand fill you with contentment, He is pleased. He takes pleasure in you. You are His delight. Giving you peace, comfort, and a sense of knowing that you belong to Him is a simple thing for Him.

Take a moment today and step away from the busyness of life. Take notice and fully experience some of those things you enjoy most. Then share that special joy with Him.

LORD, THANK YOU FOR THE SIMPLE THINGS THAT BRING PLEASURE TO MY DAY. I ENJOY EACH GIFT YOU'VE GIVEN ME. I INVITE YOU TO SHARE THOSE MOMENTS WITH ME TODAY. AMEN.

No Condemnation

Therefore there is now no condemnation at all for those who are in Christ Jesus.

ROMANS 8:1 NASB

There is no condemnation for you who are in Christ Jesus. This means there is no room for guilt or blame in your life. Even when you do things that make you feel like you have failed God, yourself, or others, your standing before God does not change. When you are in Christ, you are clothed in the clean, holy robes of God's Son. When God looks at you, He doesn't see the sins you've committed or the things you haven't done; He sees His holy, blameless Son.

How is this possible? It's possible because Christ died in your place. The sins that would have condemned you in God's holy court were placed on Christ's shoulders and buried with Him. They have no hold over you anymore. So let go of your guilt and regret. Acknowledge that Christ's work on the cross was enough to cleanse and purify you before a holy God. And live in the freedom of the knowledge that no one and nothing can condemn you. Christ has stood in your place so that you can come boldly before the Father in the clean robes that have been washed in the blood of the Lamb. Ask for and claim His forgiveness in your life.

LORD, THANK YOU THAT I AM NOT AND CANNOT BE CONDEMNED BECAUSE I AM IN CHRIST. HELP ME TO MORE FULLY UNDERSTAND WHAT CHRIST DID FOR ME ON THE CROSS SO THAT I CAN LET GO OF THE GUILT AND BLAME I SO OFTEN CARRY.

Guided into Truth

But when he, the Spirit of truth, comes, he will guide you into all the truth. He will not speak on his own; he will speak only what he hears, and he will tell you what is yet to come.

John 16:13 NIV

Isn't it amazing to realize the Spirit of God is guiding you, even now? He's like the rudder on a ship, nudging it in the direction it needs to go. The Holy Spirit is gentle and comforting, but He always aims you toward truth, for life is found in truth alone. That's why He's so keen on playing the leader while you do the following. Left to your own devices, you might veer off course.

So many people are aiming themselves toward happiness instead of following the Spirit's lead toward truth. What good would it do you if you found one but missed the other?

Today, yield to the Holy Spirit. Follow His course. Relinquish yourself to the sovereign hand of God. He wants the very best for you and is the only one capable of bringing you into the fullness of His truth.

FATHER, THANK YOU FOR THE REMINDER THAT THIS CHRISTIAN WALK ISN'T JUST ABOUT MY HAPPINESS (THOUGH I KNOW YOU WANT ME TO EXPERIENCE FULLNESS OF JOY). IT'S ABOUT FINDING TRUTH IN YOU. GUIDE ME, HOLY SPIRIT; NUDGE ME IN THE DIRECTION I NEED TO GO. AMEN.